D0894559

Faberzhe, K Faberge, 1846-192
Debrett's Peerage, in associati
3 3029 00729 0117

CENTRAL

SACRAMENTO PUBLIC LIBRARY
SACRAMENTO, CALIFORNIA

FABERGÉ

1846-1920

FRONT OF JACKET & FRONTISPIECE *Left to right* E6, F5, A26, A20, A16

BACK OF JACKET Enamel chart showing colours and *guilloché* patterns used in the Fabergé workshops

Goldsmith to the Imperial Court of Russia

FABERGÉ

1846-1920

*An International Loan Exhibition assembled
on the occasion of the Queen's Silver Jubilee
and including objects from the Royal Collection
at Sandringham*

23 June – 25 September 1977

*Debrett's Peerage Ltd. in association with
the Victoria and Albert Museum*

Contents

© A. Kenneth Snowman 1977

This catalogue is published by
Debrett's Peerage Ltd, 23 Mossop St, London SW3
for the Victoria and Albert Museum

Designed by Humphrey Stone and produced by
The Compton Press Ltd, The Old Brewery,
Tisbury, Salisbury, Wiltshire.
Colour printing by Harrison & Sons (London) Ltd.,
by appointment to Her Majesty the Queen,
Printers.

Photograph Acknowledgements

All photographs of objects owned by Her Majesty
the Queen are reproduced by her gracious permission.
In addition photographs previously used in
The Art of Carl Fabergé by A. Kenneth Snowman
are by kind permission of Faber and Faber,
and those from *Peter Carl Fabergé* by H. C. Bainbridge
by kind permission of B. T. Batsford Ltd. Photographs
of objects from the Forbes Magazine Collection are
also reproduced with their kind permission. We would
like to thank Prudence Cummings Associates
and Messrs. A. C. Cooper for all their work
on this production.

Foreword

In 1949 and again in 1953, on the occasion of the Queen's Coronation, Kenneth Snowman organised the first comprehensive exhibitions ever held in this country of the work of the great goldsmith Carl Fabergé. On those occasions the exhibitions were held at Wartski, then in Regent Street, and included many loans from the Royal Collection. The growth of interest in Fabergé since then is accurately reflected in the fact that Mr Snowman's definitive account of his work, which originally appeared in 1953, went into a second edition in 1955, an enlarged edition in 1962, and a fourth edition in 1964, with reprints both in 1968 and 1974. Nothing, therefore, would seem more appropriate than that Mr Snowman should organise a major loan exhibition of Fabergé to mark the Silver Jubilee of Her Majesty The Queen. The conception, choice and arrangement of exhibits and catalogue we owe entirely to his knowledge and enthusiasm. The design of the exhibition, a challenging task, has been the responsibility of Paul Williams of our Design Section and many others in the Museum have also been involved, principally members of our Exhibition Section and of the Department of Metalwork.

The choice of Fabergé for Jubilee Year is also appropriate because of the sustained interest in his work by the Royal Family. Initiated by the direct patronage of King Edward VII and Queen Alexandra, who introduced Queen Victoria to the work, it flourished under Queen Mary who made her own remarkable collection and is continued in the present generation by those contemporary collectors, Her Majesty The Queen, Queen Elizabeth The Queen Mother, and H.R.H. The Prince of Wales. Their objects form the core of the present exhibition. We wish to express our very real gratitude to Her Majesty The Queen and Queen Elizabeth The Queen Mother for their generosity and to Geoffrey de Bellaigue, Surveyor of The Queen's Works of Art for his ready co-operation at all points of the enterprise. For some the art of Fabergé may well seem trivial, a pandering to *fin de siècle* decadence as epitomised by late Victorian and Edwardian England and the last years of Tsarist rule in pre-revolutionary Russia. Such an attitude is understandable in a more egalitarian age with its dismissive regard toward *objets de luxe*. But such a position, if applied consistently to the decorative arts, would rob us of a vast number of its most remarkable creations.

Fabergé is almost the last expression of court art within the European tradition which brings with it a passionate conviction of the importance of craftsmanship and inventiveness of design, aligned to a celebration of the virtues of wit and fantasy applied to everyday objects, that still has a relevance to the design of today.

ROY STRONG
Director

Peter Carl Fabergé sorting a parcel of loose stones, photographed by Hugo Oeberg, one of his designers in St Petersburg.

Introduction

The impact of a restless imagination expressing itself in a variety of exotic materials in a remote city on the very fringe of Europe was to prove irresistible to an Edwardian society which was always ready to accept any addition to the accoutrements of good living.

The spell was finally cast in 1900 when, for the first time, Paris, and thus Europe, saw for itself at the Exposition Internationale Universelle, the magic that was being distilled in St Petersburg by the diligent and enterprising Carl Fabergé. The world has not emerged from this spell and the potion is as heady today and far more widely absorbed than ever before.

The Jubilee has provided a happy occasion to examine again and ask ourselves just why these confections prepared for a pampered society still obstinately retain their hold on our imagination.

There are those who do not find it possible to accept some of the more frankly prettified pastiches of mainly the French eighteenth century, but there stands nevertheless a core of individual achievement which holds a merited place in the history of the applied arts of the nineteenth century. *Edelkitsch* some of it may be, but it is not to be dismissed and has become a significant part of our European heritage.

We can now recognize in his considerable repertoire many examples which, it is difficult to believe, were not designed and made a generation later. His was very much a pioneering spirit.

Enough years have passed to appreciate the stir that the objects he made must have aroused when they were first seen. Far more ambitious because more varied than any jeweller since the eighteenth cen-tury, his position has become, in our own time, unassailable. A house-style is now distinctly recognizable throughout his *oeuvre*.

This present offering, including as it does a generous part of Queen Alexandra's own collection, affords us a rare opportunity to admire a very personal anthology assembled with affection and in a climate entirely free from economic or speculative pressure.

It will, I hope, help to demonstrate the affable spirit in which these objects were originally created – an uncomplicated desire to give pleasure.

Queen Alexandra was the sister of the Dowager Empress Marie Feodorovna and it was largely through this relationship of two Danish Princesses that the custom grew of finding a small animal carving in natural stone, or a flower study poised in a rock crystal pot, which appears, by a stratagem of the lapidary, to be filled with water, to add to the collection at Sandringham House.

As Henry Bainbridge has said, we had in England 'just the right King on the throne, with just the right experience behind him, just the right Queen with just the right love of simple things, such as animals and flowers'.

During the opening years of the century when the craftsmen were actually producing these objects, the cost was such that, though never cheap, the articles would not offend by a noisy display of too much money spent – that, I believe, is why this very personal collection makes such a seemly and cared-for impression. In this context I should like to recall the words of Sir Sacheverell Sitwell who, in his Foreword to the catalogue of the Coronation Exhibition of Fabergé's

A view of the Moscow workshops. The youth of some of Fabergé's staff is remarkable.

work held at Wartski in 1953, and which included many of the Sandringham objects, wrote:

But it is to the Sandringham Collection that one returns again. There are the objects belonging to the beautiful Queen Alexandra, no longer, then, a young woman, during the decade when she was Queen. They are not, even, objects in the most precious materials, but little toys and *objets de virtu*. The whole reason of the collection must lie in the fact that the Dowager-Empress was her sister. It was on visits to Russia that King Edward VII and Queen Alexandra saw objects from Fabergé's workshops and conceived a taste for them. Later, King Edward fell a victim to the Russian habit and commissioned presents from Fabergé, yearly, for Queen Alexandra. They are a perpetuation of Queen Alexandra's charm and humour which made her so beloved by all who knew her. These particular Fabergé objects are of no tragic significance at all, which makes them all the more delightful. It is a privilege to be allowed to enter the privacy of this Royal Collection of King Edward and Queen Alexandra and see the familiar objects that surrounded them. If they have a Russian flavour, then we remember that, large or small, as works of Fabergé the great craftsman and jeweller, they deserve to be remembered beside the Russian music and Russian novels of their day.

Henry Bainbridge managed what one hesitates to call the London branch of Fabergé's; one should perhaps find a more exalted word for what was in effect a private salon opened for the personal convenience of the Royal Family and their immediate entourage of friends. It was up in this eyrie in 48 Dover Street that the King's friend Mrs George Keppel actually suggested making portrait models of some of the favourite animals and pets for the Queen's collection 'if the King will give his permission'. The following day Bainbridge received a telegram from Sandringham 'The King agrees'.

Thus it was that Mr Bainbridge (concealed for some obscure reason, like a latterday Polonius, behind a hedge!) was able to record

The interior of the St Petersburg shop.

how on December 8th 1907, he observed His Majesty, encased in a tight-fitting overcoat and beneath what appeared to be a mini cricket cap, leading his guests after luncheon from Sandringham House across the lawn to Queen Alexandra's Dairy.

The purpose of this pilgrimage was to examine the display of wax models which a group of artists from St Petersburg had been preparing during the previous month. Included in this working party was Boris Froedman-Cluzel together with the Swiss, Frank Lutiger.

When the *maquettes* arrived at St Petersburg, careful selections were made as to the most suitable materials for the final carving.

These studies of animals, birds, insects and fish can be clearly divided into two types. Some are taken directly from nature and are very carefully finished with every hair in place so to speak. The others

A bust of Carl
Fabergé by Joseph
Limburg, 1903.

that an object wanting in this respect cannot be from the hands of the Fabergé workmasters.

We know how stern a critic he was and that a substantial proportion of the pieces made were never allowed to see the light of day.

Fabergé's contribution to the decorative arts of the late nineteenth and early twentieth centuries was the result of his own private Russian Revolution. He decreed that the emphasis previously concentrated on the sheer value of the material used should be shifted, without compromise, on to the craftsmanship devoted to a given object.

Looking back upon this personal credo, he has referred, with disdain, to the leading European jewellers as merchants and not artist-jewellers. He is reported in *Stolitza y Usadba* (Town and Country), St Petersburg, January 15th, 1914, to have said 'Expensive things interest me little if the value is merely in so many diamonds or pearls.'

The late Queen Mary, a redoubtable and highly informed connoisseur, added many of the more dramatic subjects to the Royal Collection, such as the Colonnade Egg (F 3) and the miniature *écritoire* in Louis XVI taste (K 4), and Queen Elizabeth The Queen Mother, who always shared with the late King George VI, a very lively enthusiasm for this work, has assembled her own beautiful group of objects, among which the bunch of wild flowers in a vase with an enamelled gem-set honey bee is outstanding (F 9).

The Queen herself continues this family tradition as the Exhibition vividly demonstrates and has readily and generously made the Royal Collection available so that all those interested may examine and enjoy the best work of one of the world's last great artist-designers.

There are, in this exhibition, several objects with which Fabergé must have been particularly pleased – not necessarily the most elaborate or costly, but ones exemplifying the sort of glamour we have come to associate with his name. I have in mind the exquisitely carved agate pumpkin box (J 10) with its echoes, some distance away, of eighteenth-century Dresden, the blue enamelled cigarette case wound round by its glittering diamond snake, designed with all the concentration of a Beardsley drawing, and having in addition such a fascinating history

are conventionalized essays designed to bring out some particular characteristic such as the chubby bulk of an elephant or a pig, the nervous watchful agility of a frog or the sheer clumsiness of a pelican.

Inevitably, the most successful of the conventionalized figures portray subjects which manifest some sort of oddity or quirk in real life, subjects which in fact would attract the cartoonist in any medium.

The purpurine elephant in this exhibition was clearly a source of enormous pleasure to the sculptor who designed it and indeed, before close examination, it appears simply to be a heavy bright crimson ball (C 15). Quality was sought at all times. So much so, it is safe to assume

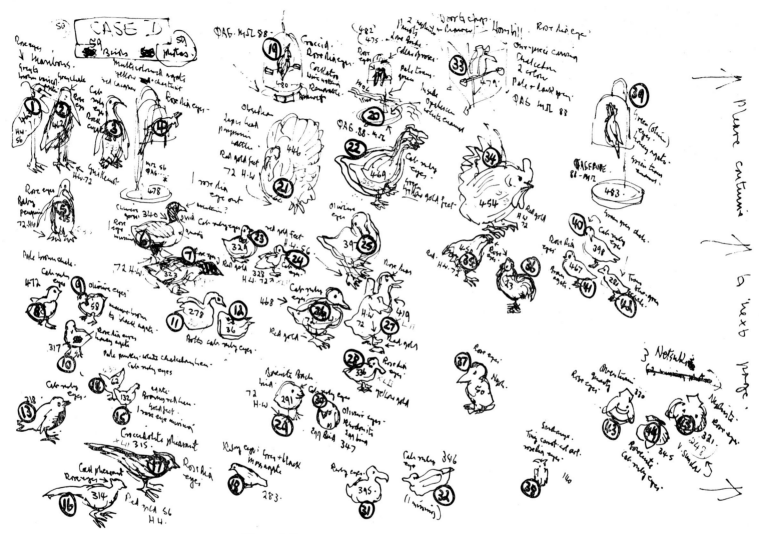

The Sandringham birds, sketches made by A. Kenneth Snowman during his work on the Royal Collection for this exhibition.

(K**2**), the score of flower studies which together present a twinkling green-house-cum-*Schatzkammer*, the aviary of fifty-nine sculptured birds, the sherry-agate negro head in the form of a bowl (R**25**) and too many of the animal carvings to enumerate here. Perhaps a passing reference should be made to the lively little carving of an owl in carrot-coloured agate and which stands only five eighths of an inch high. Two greatly enlarged coloured photographs in the catalogue give an idea of just how much observed detail it was possible for a talented sculptor to concentrate into a work on even such a tiny scale (D**38**).

It is a special pleasure to see again the sensational basket of lilies of the valley (M**9**) formerly the favourite possession of that very considerable human being and friend, Matilda Gray. How gratifying also to have once again, under the same roof, the Imperial Presentation Box in the Forbes Magazine collection (O**14**) and the Coronation Egg (O**1**) which were the gifts exchanged by the Tsar and Tsarina on Easter Day 1897.

Apart from these two important private collections, the museums of America have been extremely generous and visitors to the exhibition will acknowledge a deep debt of gratitude to the Cleveland Museum of Art, the Virginia Museum, Richmond and the Walters Art Gallery in Baltimore.

In setting out this exhibition I have included a great deal of material, recognizing that these Victorian and Edwardian souvenirs were never intended to be regarded as holy relics, to be displayed individually and with formal reverence. On the contrary they are at their best when viewed in groups – a glance at any of the photographs of the period which show the tables and bureaux in the Russian Palaces and Sandringham, laden with rows of enamelled miniature frames, amply confirms this view. Nineteen small carvings of dogs of varied species for example are shown as an independent group representing, as it were, Fabergé's essay on the dog.

My only regret is that my father, Emanuel Snowman, MVO, OBE, did not live to enjoy this, the first comprehensive exhibition of Fabergé's work to be held in a national museum, having himself done

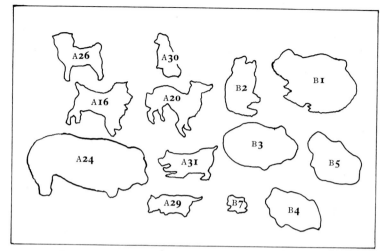

OPPOSITE ▲

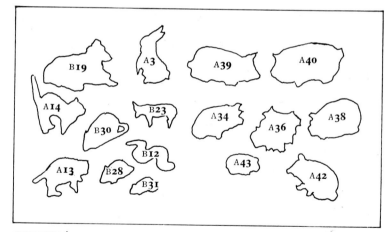

OVERLEAF ▲

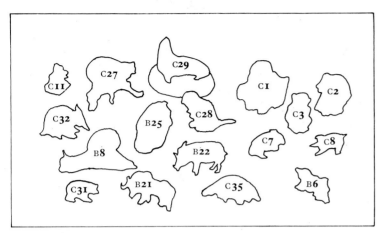

OVERLEAF ▲

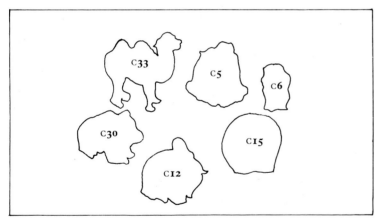

OPPOSITE   *Left* ▲   *Right* D38 (two views)

so much, so enthusiastically, to bring it before the public. He would have been especially happy to have seen again the enchanting Peacock Egg which he brought over from Russia, with so many other treasures, in the twenties (O **10**).

I should like to express my thanks to Dr Roy Strong for having wholeheartedly and unhesitatingly accepted the idea of this exhibition in the first place.

I am grateful to the lapidaries George Bull-Diamond, Brian Lloyd and Peter Rome and to Dr Michael Brambell and Peter Olney, the Curators of respectively, Mammals and Birds at the London Zoo, and to Michael Boorer of the Zoological Society of London, for their invaluable advice. Miss Frances Dimond, from her Round Tower at Windsor, has kept me supplied with wonderfully detailed answers to all my photographic queries.

I count myself lucky in having had at all times the benefit of practical and friendly help from Michael Darby, Paul Williams and Sue Runyard at the Museum. My tireless wife Sallie, David Edmond and Geoffrey Munn have been indispensable in matters of research, and I have received much practical assistance from Marina Bowater, Beryl Inglis, the Archduke Dr Geza von Habsburg and Eugene Mollo. I very much want to thank June Trager for her unfailing patience and industry in helping to assemble the material for this catalogue; my old friend Harold Brooks-Baker is responsible for having secured Julian Berry, Humphrey Stone, Malcolm Rice and Diana Keith Neal who have designed and prepared it with such care.

This event was conceived in the first instance as, quite simply, a Compliment to the Queen on Her Silver Jubilee and it is our hope that this goal may have been achieved.

A. KENNETH SNOWMAN

Chronology

1842   Firm established by Gustav in Bolshaya Morskaya Street in St Petersburg.

1846   Peter Carl Fabergé born in St Petersburg on 30th May. Baptized in the Protestant Church.

1870   Fabergé takes control of the firm at the age of twenty-four. New ground-floor premises taken opposite original basement, now closed.

1872   Fabergé marries Augusta Julia Jacobs.

1882   Fabergé's younger brother Agathon arrives from Dresden to join the firm at the age of twenty.
The House exhibits for first time at Pan-Russian Exhibition in Moscow, and wins a Gold Medal.

1884   First Imperial Easter Egg presented to the Empress Marie Feodorovna.
Alexander III grants his Royal Warrant to the House of Fabergé in 1884 or 1885.

1885   House awarded Gold Medal at Nuremberg Fine Art Exhibition for gold replicas of Scythian Treasure.

1886   Michael Perchin joins the firm.

1888   Special Diploma received at Northern Exhibition in Copenhagen; the House was *hors concours*, being represented on the jury.

Gustav Petrovitch Fabergé and his wife, parents of Carl Fabergé, photographed in Dresden.

1890　St Petersburg premises doubled in size. Branch opened in Odessa.

1893　Death of Gustav Fabergé in Dresden on his seventy-ninth birthday. Art Nouveau movement now launched in Europe.

1894　Death of Alexander III on 1st November.
Marriage of Nicholas II on 7th December.
Eugène Fabergé joins the firm.

1895　Death of Fabergé's brother Agathon at age of thirty-three.

1896　Coronation of Nicholas II.
House awarded State Emblem at Pan-Russian Exhibition at Nijny-Novgorod.
The *Kokoshnik* was almost certainly adopted as State mark for gold and silver throughout Russia in 1896.

1897　Granted Royal Warrant by Court of Sweden and Norway.

1898　Premises bought at 24 Morskaya Street and reconstruction started.

1900　Removal to Morskaya Street.
Imperial Eggs exhibited for first time at the Paris 'Exposition Internationale Universelle'. Carl Fabergé, member of jury, acclaimed *Maître* and decorated with Légion d'Honneur.

1901　Death of Eric Kollin.

1903　Arthur Bowe sent from Moscow to London to start up business for Fabergé from Berners Hotel.
Death of Michael Perchin; workshop taken over by his chief assistant, Henrik Wigström.
Death of August Holmström, succeeded by his son Albert.

Fabergé's shop in Moscow.

1904　Birth of Tsarevitch.
Fabergé invited to visit King Chulalongkorn of Siam.
London branch removes to Portman House, Duke Street, Grosvenor Square. Objects by Fabergé exhibited for first time in England by Lady Paget at an Albert Hall bazaar in aid of Royal Hospital for Children.

1906　London branch removes to 48 Dover Street under Nicholas Fabergé and H. C. Bainbridge.
Beginning of business connections with Siam, India and China.

1907 Artists working at Sandringham finish models for stone animal carvings.

Baron Foelkersam's *Inventaire de l'Argenterie* published, in which he writes: 'This firm (Fabergé), which is one of the best and most famous in the world, is renowned above all for its *objets d'art*. Articles made in Fabergé's workshops are known for their technical excellence, especially as regards enamelling, stone polishing and engraving.'

1908 Carl Fabergé arrives in London from St Petersburg to see Dover Street premises on 29th January, and leaves hurriedly the same day for Paris when informed that he would be expected to seek audience with Queen Alexandra.

1911 London branch moves to 173 New Bond Street.
Nicholas II commissions Fabergé to carve miniature stone figures of Empress's Cossack Bodyguard.

1913 Tercentenary of Romanov rule brings about revival of Russian Mediaevalism in applied arts known as 'Old Russian Style'.

1915 Bond Street shop closes down. Death of August Höllming.

1916 Death of Julius Rappoport.

1917 Russian Revolution.
The House closes for a short period at beginning of Revolution.

1918 Firm finally closed down by Bolsheviks.
Carl Fabergé escapes in September via Riga, Berlin, Frankfurt and Homburg to Wiesbaden as a courier attached to the British Embassy.

Carl Fabergé at the Imperial Hotel, Wiesbaden in May 1920 after his escape from Russia and shortly before his death.

1920 Carl Fabergé arrives at Lausanne in June.
Dies on 24th September at the Hotel Bellevue, La Rosiaz.

1929 Eugène brings his father's remains from Lausanne Crematorium to Cannes, and buries them in the grave with his mother. He sets up tombstone in black Swedish porphyry bearing this inscription:

CHARLES FABERGÉ
joaillier de la Cour de Russie
né 18 mai 1846 à St Petersbourg
décédé 24 septembre 1920 à Lausanne

AUGUSTA FABERGÉ
née JACOBS
née 25 decembre 1851 (vieux style) à Tsarskoé Selo
décédée 27 janvier 1925 (nouveau style) à Cannes

A Note on the Metals, Enamels and Stones used by Fabergé

Taking the precious metals first, it is clear that to Fabergé the colour of the gold or silver, as well as the precise shade of the enamel or stone, was a matter of the most deliberate consideration.

Coloured Golds There are two methods of obtaining coloured golds, and Fabergé employed both. The metal used by goldsmiths is generally an alloy because pure 24 carat gold, although used occasionally for small trinkets, is much too soft for ordinary practical purposes. In the gold most often used by Fabergé (56 corresponding to our 14 carat), the nature of the metal added to complete the alloy (10 parts to 14 in the case of 14 carat) determines the final colour of the gold.

The colour of the gold alloy is controlled by the precise proportions of pure gold, and mainly pure copper and fine silver; for some special shades other metals, such as pure nickel or palladium, may be introduced. Pure gold combined with fine silver gives a green gold, and with pure copper, a red gold.

The numerous variations of the alloy enable the goldsmith to produce yellow, green, red and white golds in very many degrees of intensity, as well as certain even more *recherché* effects such as blue, orange and grey golds. In the main, however, Fabergé confined his attention to the more usual colours.

The other method of colouring gold, less frequently employed in Morskaya Street, is simply to tint it after the work is finished. It is sometimes difficult to discern which technique has been adopted without disturbing the surface of the metal.

The *quatre-couleur* technique of the eighteenth-century goldsmiths in France was developed to a surprising extent in the St Petersburg *ateliers*, and this was often combined with the use of enamels or stones to give increased point to the subtle variations between the differently-coloured golds.

Fabergé very effectively combined dull or matt golds with polished gold of another colour; for instance a chiselled swag would be executed in matt green gold and the small bows and ties in polished red gold.

Other Metals As well as making a great deal of polished silverware, mostly in the Moscow House, Fabergé was one of the first to make extensive use of oxidized silver, and produce a large quantity of *surtouts-de-table, bratini*, bowls and samovar sets in this medium. The tea service (s 4) provides a good example of the technique.

Enamels Fabergé's superb enamelling techniques are perhaps the most important aspect of his work. Enamelling is a complex process, fraught with difficulties and it is necessary for the layman to understand the ancient technique before being able to comprehend the extent to which Fabergé stretched and embroidered on the process. He thus subjected his workmasters to a continuous rigorous test of their skills in order to achieve more exotic and subtle effects in a manner only attempted by French eighteenth century goldsmiths.

Enamelling in the simplest sense is 'a semi-opaque variety of glass, applied by fusion to metallic surfaces'. The word 'fusion' is the key to the whole operation. For enamel to become malleable, it has to be heated to a certain temperature, and it is precisely this heating that creates the problems that so consistently defeat the modern craftsman. The finest translucent enamel has to be brought up to a heat of about 600 degrees centigrade – Fabergé's enamellers normally worked at temperatures varying between 700 and 800 degrees; at such tremendous heat, it is obvious that if there has been any slight error or miscalculation in the preparation of the actual enamel or flux, or if the alloy of the metal plate used is not entirely suited to the enamel covering it, disaster, swift and sure, will undoubtedly follow.

In practice, it is astonishing to learn how much heat 14 carat gold, for example, can withstand without coming to grief. It is usually necessary to apply enamel to a part of an object already worked by the goldsmith, and even if the temperature inside the 'muffle' of the kiln were raised to 1,000 degrees centigrade, the metal would emerge from its ordeal by fire unscathed, as about 1,200 degrees would be needed to affect a gold of this hardness. It is seldom necessary to risk passing gems through the fire, the technique being to cut out the raised settings in advance, then, when the enamel has been applied, the stones may be inserted and the settings closed round to secure them.

Characteristics of Fabergé enamelling are the even quality and smoothness of its texture. He specialised in what is known as *en plein* enamelling; this means the smooth covering of comparatively large surfaces or fields. This type of work allows for no margin of error. But perhaps the key to Fabergé's use of enamel was his subtle combination of techniques. Rather in the way he used matt and burnished coloured gold surfaces together, so he contrasted opaque and translucent enamel, the latter with patterns engraved underneath.

Opaque enamel usually requires a lower temperature than translucent, about 300 degrees sufficing. This lower temperature firing is known as '*petit feu*' as opposed to '*grand feu*'.

Translucent enamelling involves the firing of transparent layers of enamel, the fusibility of each carefully matched, on a prepared metal surface. In Fabergé's work this area is generally engine-turned (or sometimes engraved by hand), and is known as a *guilloché* surface.

The enamel firing kiln in the Fabergé workshops.

Each layer of enamel, and there may be as many as five or six, has to be baked separately. Sometimes gold leaf patterns known as *paillons* or painted decorations or scenes appear beneath the surface of such enamels: this lovely effect is obtained by applying and firing the gold leaf or the enamel on to an already fired enamel surface before the top sealing layer of enamel is in turn applied and fired. When the enamel has been baked, it requires careful polishing with a wooden wheel in order to smooth down any irregularities on the surface; this is a highly specialized and extremely laborious operation and one without which the finished article will lack that distinction we have come to connect with Fabergé's work. The enamel is then finished off with the buff.

The characteristic milky quality of some of the translucent enamels, and especially the white, a rich fullness difficult to describe on paper but easy to recognize in reality, was obtained by a mixture made up in the proportion of four to six parts of transparent, to one part of opaque enamel, producing a semi-opaque material. This enamel is generally described as *opalescent*.

Another feature of some of his enamel pieces is the way the colour appears to alter as the object is turned very slightly; this effect was brought about by simply varying the colours of the layers of enamel. A pale flame-coloured layer of semi-transparent enamel beneath one or more layers of white transparent enamel imparts a particularly enchanting lustre – the round box in the Sandringham Collection (H8) is an excellent instance of this technique. Also the effect of the light on the separate crystals of which the enamel is composed often gives the impression of a second colour. This variation in colour combined with painting beneath the top surface of enamel is illustrated very well in the Easter Egg made for Barbara Kelch (F1). Add to these variations in colour, the colour and engraved pattern of the gold *guilloché* field – the carcass of the Egg itself, which can be seen through the layers of warm semi-transparent enamel, sometimes indistinctly, at other times very clearly, depending upon the angle of vision and the light, and we begin to get some conception of the thought and careful planning that went into the creation of such an object.

Cloisonné Enamel: Fabergé decorated many silver and silver-gilt pieces with *cloisonné* enamels. He preferred a pastel palette to the cruder blues and reds chosen by most Russian nineteenth century silversmiths. A network of raised metal enclosures is soldered to the body of the object which is to be treated. The enamels are poured into these *cloisons*, the metal tops of which remain exposed, allowing the different colours in each one to be distinctly shown, serving as jewels in separate settings or collets. There are several examples in case s.

Stones The lapidaries working in Russia found everything in their favour; the richest imaginable variety of natural resources was, practically speaking, on their doorstep, from the vivid Siberian emerald to the grey jasper of Kalgan. This astonishing abundance of mineral deposits to be found in the Urals, the Caucasus, Siberia, and elsewhere, must have been a source of great satisfaction to Fabergé, and time and time again he is able to transmit to us his own pleasure in some particularly choice stone by means of an animal carving, or a dish or box.

As far as *precious stones* were concerned, he rarely used these unless the purely decorative demands of the particular object called for them. Sapphires, rubies and emeralds were most frequently used *en cabochon*, and nine times out of ten the diamonds he used were rose-cut; he confined his use of brilliant diamonds to specially commissioned and Imperial pieces. Rose-cut diamonds set next to enamel or stone become part of the whole, whereas there is sometimes a danger that brilliant-cut stones, being so much brighter, might appear out of tone unless steps were taken, such as specially designed settings, to prevent this.

Semi-precious gem stones were used a great deal, especially moonstones, cabochon garnets, olivines and stained chalcedonies cut *cabochon* known as Mecca stones.

The other *hardstones* for carving to which he seems to have been most attracted were rock crystal, jade, bowenite, agate, jasper, rhodonite and quartz, aventurine, lapis lazuli and pale green flecked and opalescent amazonite.

A word or two about the special properties of some of these stones might be useful in this context. There are, strictly speaking, only two varieties of jade, nephrite and jadeite; both were used by Fabergé, nephrite a very great deal, jadeite only very occasionally. The nephrite he used was the dark green stone found in Siberia. The pale yellow-green stone usually described as 'pale jade' is not a jade at all, but a hard form of serpentine known as bowenite; known, that is to say, since 1822 when G. T. Bowen published his findings in the American *Journal of Science*. Until that time, this stone was erroneously thought to be nephrite. Apart from Rhode Island, U.S.A., where Bowen found it, this form of serpentine is also present in Afghanistan, from which source, doubtless, Fabergé had the stone imported.

Rhodonite or orletz, to give it its Russian name, is one of the most beautiful of all the natural stones; it was mined at Ekaterinburg and is characterized by its warm rose colour.

Obsidian, a natural volcanic glass of a grey-black colour which imparts a soft velvety sheen when polished, was peculiarly suited to the carving of animals.

Aventurine quartz, a tawny material mined in the Altai Mountains, also has a particularly attractive surface owing to the gold spangles which become evident when it is polished.

Besides the many natural stones available to the firm, a deep crimson material known as *purpurine* was frequently used with great effect. A worker in the Imperial Glass Factory in St Petersburg, named Petouchov, discovered the secret of its manufacture. A similar process was known in the eighteenth century to the lapidaries of Murano, to whom also must go the credit for the invention of aventurine glass or 'goldstone'.

The purpurine-like substance found in Italian work however, is considerably lighter both in colour and weight; this is probably due to a smaller proportion of lead in its composition than that used by Petouchov.

The manufacture of purpurine would appear to have been brought about by the crystallization of a lead chromate in a glass matrix. It is a material of great beauty both on account of the intensity and depth of its *sang de boeuf* colour and its spangled glassy texture. The Fabergé workshops seem to have had the exclusive use of this attractive material.

Maquettes: before starting up with the wheel on a freshly ground piece of stone, the sculptor would generally have before him a wax or plaster model of the subject from which to work. The lapidaries would not necessarily carry out their own ideas; there were about twenty artists and designers in Fabergé's drawing-studio, and it was here that these preliminary wax figures were modelled.

The Studio photographed by Nicholas Fabergé, where most of the twenty-five or so designers worked. Alexander Fabergé is seen on the extreme left, Eugène stands at the back of the room, Oscar May is seated in front of him. In the case at the back the original wax models used for the animal carvings are seen.

A wax model, typical of the studies from which the Fabergé artists carved the hardstone animals.

In some cases – the Sandringham series is an obvious example – the original modelling from nature would be done on the spot and the carving carried out in the St Petersburg workshop.

Woods He had a nice appreciation of the different woods to be found in and around Russia. Karelian birch, palisander, and holly wood in particular were used for many diverse objects including cigarette-cases, miniature frames, and even bell-pushes.

The cases in which Fabergé pieces were delivered were generally made of wood – for the most part, polished white holly wood; they were beautifully made and provided a worthy setting for a precious gift.

Marks and Standards

State marks Up to the year 1896, St Petersburg and Moscow each had their own separate cyphers which are easily distinguishable. St Petersburg, where the bulk of Fabergé's vitrine objects were made, had as the gold mark of the city, two crossed anchors intersected vertically by a sceptre.

Moscow, where a much more commercial business was carried on, had as the city gold mark a Saint George and Dragon.

In 1896 both St Petersburg and Moscow, and for that matter the other manufacturing centres in Russia, abandoned their separate gold marks and adopted a woman's head seen in profile wearing the traditional head-dress known as a *Kokoshnik*.

Gold and Silver Standards The Russian gold standards in general use at this time were reckoned in *zolotniks* in the same way as ours are expressed in carats. The gold alloy of 96 parts, contains in Fabergé's objects, either 56 or 72 *zolotniks* of pure gold, just as our alloy of 24

parts, or carats, contains a certain proportion of pure gold, 9, 18 or 22 parts being the most common. It is useful to remember that the 96 parts of the Russian alloy correspond to the 24 parts of the English alloy – a ratio of 4 to 1. Hence, if the Russian gold standards (56 and 72 *zolotniks*, for instance) are divided by 4, the results given represent the English standard equivalents (14 and 18 carats respectively).

The Russian standards for silver are also indicated by the number of *zolotniks* of pure silver out of 96 *zolotniks* of alloy. The most frequently found proportions are 84 and 88, although it is not altogether uncommon to find objects stamped 91. The English 'sterling' standard requires that at least 925 parts out of a total of 1000 parts of silver alloy be pure silver. By proportional calculation it thus becomes clear that while the Russian standards 84 and 88 are below the English standard for sterling silver, the standard 91 is above.

See p. 25 for identification of gold and silver marks on objects in the exhibition.

Makers' Marks Most, but by no means all, Fabergé objects bear some sort of mark of the House. The first obvious exceptions to this rule are the carvings in stone; a mark, even if practicable, would almost always disturb the surface beauty of such pieces, and when a signature of some sort is found, for example on the under-surface of a stone animal, this is tantamount to a proclamation that this carving is not by Fabergé at all.

The form of the signature stamped or engraved on an object usually reveals its origin of manufacture; those pieces made in St Petersburg simply bear the name Fabergé in Russian characters, 'ФАБЕРЖЕ', without any initial, usually followed, or preceded, by the workmaster's initials. Sometimes a piece will be found to bear only the House name or only the workmaster's initials. Objects made in St Petersburg are sometimes marked. К.Ф. Most workmasters' initials appear in Roman letters but some are stamped in Russian characters, for example 'I.P.' for Julius Rappoport.

The pieces made in *Moscow* are marked with the signature К. ФАБЕРЖЕ beneath an Imperial double-headed eagle, or, as in St Petersburg, they too are simply stamped with the initials К.Ф. as are those made in Odessa and Kiev, where Fabergé had branches and small workshops.

The full Moscow mark signifies that the firm held the Royal Warrant of Appointment and was entitled to stamp the Imperial cypher above the House name.

Pieces made in St Petersburg, however, were treated differently. Fabergé felt that credit should be given to the particular workmaster responsible for the work and that, in fact, it was not an anonymous product of the House, but the original work of the man whose initials it bore, and that man, whether he was Perchin, Wigström or any of the others, was clearly not a Warrant holder.

It was in this characteristically generous way that the workmaster was recognized by Fabergé, as being in charge of a carefully selected group of talented craftsmen, who was entitled to sign his own creation.

St Petersburg gold mark showing firm's name, workmaster's initials, sometimes upside down, and a high grade gold mark, 72.

Fabergé's Workmasters and their Marks

Erik August Kollin	E.K.
Michael Evlampievich Perchin	M.П.
Henrik Wigström	H.W.
Julius Alexandrovitch Rappoport	I.P.
August Wilhelm Holmström	A.H.
Alfred Thielemann	A.T.
August Fredrik Hollming	A★H
Johan Viktor Aarne	B.A.
Karl Gustav Hjalmar Armfelt	Я.A.
Anders Johan Nevalainen	A.N.
Gabriel Niukkanen	G.N.
Philip Theodore Ringe	T.R.
Vladimir Soloviev	B.C.
Anders Michelsson	A.M.
G. Lundell	Г.Л.
Fedor Afanassiev	Ф.A.
Edward Wilhelm Schramm	E.S.
Wilhelm Reimer	W.R.
Andrej Gorianov	A.Г.
Stephan Wäkevä	S.W.
Knut Oskar Pihl	O.P.
Fedor Rückert	Ф.P.

Catalogue Notes

When the maker of an object is known, the workmaster's initials are given under the catalogue description. For example:

Signed MП

Gold marks are identified if they are those in use before the *Kokoshnik* was adopted and if the purity of the metal exceeds the normal 56 *zolotniks*. For example:

Gold marks 72 and crossed anchors.

Silver marks are treated in the same way and only noted if the purity exceeds the more usual 84 and 88 *zolotniks*. For example:

Silver marks 91 and St George and dragon.

Where no acknowledgement is made below a catalogue entry in cases K and M to S, it is to be assumed that this item forms part of a private collection.

Many of the objects shown in this exhibition are illustrated in one or other of two books on the subject of Fabergé. They are:

Peter Carl Fabergé by H. C. Bainbridge, Batsford, 1949.

The Art of Carl Fabergé by A. Kenneth Snowman, Faber, 1962.

For the sake of brevity, these are referred to in the catalogue as, respectively, HCB and AKS.

Those objects that are illustrated in colour in the catalogue have the page number on which the illustration appears at the end of the entry – viz [64].

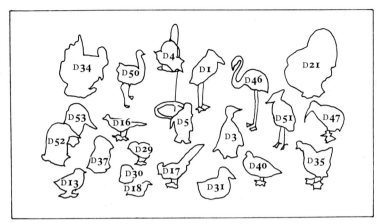

OPPOSITE ▲

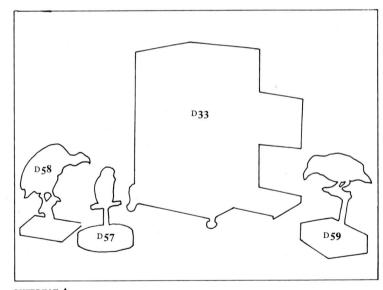

OVERLEAF ▲

CASE A

Animal carvings from the collection at Sandringham, lent by gracious permission of Her Majesty The Queen.

A1 White chalcedony RABBIT with cabochon ruby eyes; possibly a study for the White Rabbit from Alice in Wonderland from a series designed by Fabergé but now lost.
Height 2¾ inches
AKS plate 259

A2 Small dull cream chalcedony RABBIT with cabochon ruby eyes.
Height 1 3/16 inches

A3 RABBIT in translucent honey-coloured agate with rose diamond eyes. [14]
Height 1 9/16 inches

A4 Group of DOE AND THREE BABY RABBITS in translucent vari-coloured dark brown agate with rose diamond eyes.
Length 3½ inches

A5 Crouching RABBIT in translucent grey chalcedony with cabochon ruby eyes.
Height 2 inches

A6 RABBIT in rock crystal with cabochon ruby eyes.
Length 1⅞ inches

A7 Purpurine RABBIT with rose diamond eyes.
Length 1⅝ inches

A8 Amethyst RABBIT with rose diamond eyes.
Length 1¼ inches

A9 Tawny aventurine-quartz RABBIT with olivine eyes.
Height 1⅜ inches

A10 Tiny lapis lazuli RABBIT set with rose diamond eyes.
Length ¾ inch

A11 Running RABBIT in translucent white chalcedony with rose diamond eyes.
Length 1⅜ inches

A12 Tawny aventurine-quartz seated RABBIT with rose diamond eyes.
Height 1 5/16 inches

A13 Blue and brown vari-coloured agate KITTEN set with rose diamond eyes, edging sideways. [14]
Length 2 inches

A14 CAT with arched back in grey Kalgan jasper, known in Russia as *troitsk,* with emerald eyes set in yellow gold. [14]
Height 2 3/16 inches
AKS plate 250

A15 Dark brown-grey agate stylized carving of a BULLDOG, recalling the cartoon character Bonzo, set with rose diamond eyes.
Height 2¾ inches
HCB plate 73

A16 Portrait model of Edward VII's NORFOLK TERRIER 'Caesar' in white chalcedony with cabochon ruby eyes and gold bell and a translucent brown-enamelled gold collar inscribed 'I belong to the King'. [13]
Length 2¼ inches
HCB plate 95   AKS plate 255

A17 Portrait model of Queen Alexandra's favourite PEKINESE carved in pale green fluor-spar with rose diamond eyes.
    To judge from the choice of stone, readily available in this country, and the generally broad style of carving and the finish, this model is, in all probability, the work of Alfred Pocock, the only Englishman who worked for Fabergé, and who both designed and carved several of the Sandringham animals. Differing in character with Fabergé's work as a whole, it is nevertheless included here out of historical interest in this context.
Length 4½ inches
HCB plate 96

A17

A18 PEKINESE carved from dark grey banded agate with creamy striations, set with rose diamond eyes.
Length 1¾ inches

A19 POODLE carved from dark grey and white banded agate with yellow-stained cabochon chalcedony eyes.
Length 3⅛ inches
AKS colour plate XLII

A20 COLLIE in translucent brown and blue-grey agate, with cabochon ruby eyes. [13]
Length 2 11/16 inches

A21 Smooth POMERANIAN in translucent pale and darker grey chalcedony with rose diamond eyes.
Length 2 1/16 inches

A22 Stylized PUG in the Chinese taste, in warm tawny aventurine-quartz with rose diamond eyes set in gold.
Length 2 inches

A23 Seated bowenite BULLDOG with ruby eyes, wearing a gold collar set alternately with rubies and rose diamonds in separate collets, from which hangs a gold disc engraved '1st Prize' in Russian characters.
Height 1 11/16 inches

A24 Portrait model of a CLUMBER SPANIEL in pale grey chalcedony with cabochon ruby eyes. [13]
Length 4⅛ inches
HCB plate 95   AKS plate 255

A25 Striated brown agate DACHSHUND with rose diamond eyes.
Length 3 inches
AKS colour plate XLII

A26 Standing brown agate GRIFFON of haughty mien, with rose diamond eyes. [13]
Length 1⅞ inches

A27 Standing BORDER TERRIER in vari-coloured brown chalcedony with rose diamond eyes.
Length 1⅞ inches

A28 Parti-coloured translucent agate WEST HIGHLAND TERRIER with rose diamond eyes.
Length 2⅜ inches

A29 Vari-coloured brown and grey agate DACHSHUND PUPPY with rose diamond eyes, shown sniffing. [13]
Length 1⅞ inches
AKS plate 255

A30 Seated KING CHARLES SPANIEL in greenish-grey translucent chalcedony with rose diamond eyes. [13]
Height 1 7/16 inches

A31 Vari-coloured blue-grey chalcedony BORDER TERRIER, with rose diamond eyes, shown about to spring. [13]
Length 2 1/16 inches

A32 Semi-transparent striated brown agate BULLDOG with rose diamond eyes.
Length 2½ inches
AKS plate 255

A33 Seated grey-brown agate FRENCH BULLDOG with rose diamond eyes.
Height 2⅛ inches

A34 Seated PIG in white and pink aventurine-quartz with cabochon ruby eyes. [14]
Length 2⅛ inches
AKS plate 258

A35 Portrait model of a SOW in pale aventurine-quartz, with rose diamond eyes.
Length 6 inches
HCB plate 96

A36 Litter of four sleeping PIGLETS in differing tones of chalcedony, connected beneath by a gold trellis mount. [14]
Length 2 1/16 inches   Signed М.П.
AKS colour plate XXXVII illustrates a very similar group.

A37 Seated PIG in dark brown chalcedony with pale blue inclusions, with rose diamond eyes.
Length 2½ inches

A38 Standing purpurine PIG, with rose diamond eyes. [14]
Length 2⅛ inches
AKS colour plate XLII

A**39** Pink striated agate PIG with yellow and grey inclusions, with olivine eyes. [14]
Length 2¾ inches
AKS plate 256

A**40** Pinky-brown chalcedony SOW with rose diamond eyes. [14]
Length 2⅞ inches
AKS plate 256

A**41** Vari-coloured pinky-grey agate PIG with rose diamond eyes.
Length 1¾ inches
AKS plate 257

A**42** Seated vari-coloured agate PIG, with rose diamond eyes, shown scratching its ear. [14]
Length 1⅝ inches

A**43** Fat orange-brown chalcedony PIG with rose diamond eyes. [14]
Length 1⅛ inches

A**44** Bowenite PIG with cabochon ruby eyes.
Length 2 inches

A**45** Rock crystal PIG with cabochon ruby eyes in gold settings.
Height 1 1/16 inches

CASE B

Animal carvings from the collection at Sandringham lent by gracious permission of Her Majesty The Queen.

B1 Dark green Siberian nephrite FROG with large rose diamond eyes in gold settings. [13]
Length 3⅜ inches

B2 Dark red speckled jasper croaking FROG with olivine eyes. [13]
Height 2⅛ inches
AKS plate 273

B3 Bowenite FROG with large cabochon garnet eyes and rose diamond teeth set in yellow gold, designed as a box with a red gold lid enamelled opaque black and set with rose diamonds. [13]
Length 2⅝ inches   Signed M.П
AKS plate 273

B4 Three-legged TOAD carved in the style of a netsuke in chocolate brown jasper and set with olivine eyes. [13]
Length 1¾ inches

B5 Speckled grey labradorite TOAD, the stone with unusual green translucent inclusions, with cabochon ruby eyes in gold settings. Carved underneath in the manner of a netsuke. [13]
Length 1⅞ inches

B6 Siberian nephrite TOAD highly polished to express the wetness of the creature and with brilliant diamond eyes in gold settings. [15]
Length 2⅛ inches

B7 Tiny dark nephrite FROG with rose diamond eyes. [13]
Length ⅝ inch
AKS plate 227

B8 SNAIL in chalcedony of pale grey-green, the shell of translucent jasper in shades of blue-grey, rust, mauve and pastel greens. [15]
Length 3 15/16 inches
AKS plate 273

B9 Speckled brown FLAT FISH, known in Norfolk as a butt, with rose diamond eyes set in gold.
Length 2¾ inches
AKS plate 273

B10 Small SNAIL in parti-coloured cream and brown agate; a one-piece carving in cameo technique.
Length ¾ inch
AKS plate 230

B11 Dark blue-grey and pinky-brown chalcedony DOLPHIN with rose diamond eyes.
Length 2¾ inches
AKS plate 227

B12 Vari-coloured agate SNAKE, possibly an adder, with rose diamond eyes. [14]
Length 2¼ inches
AKS colour plate XLII

B13 Pale silvery-grey to pinky-brown chalcedony seated WILD BOAR with cabochon ruby eyes.
Length 3¼ inches

B14 Aventurine-quartz SHIRE HORSE with cabochon sapphire eyes in gold settings, a portrait model of Sandringham's champion 'Field Marshal'.
Length 7 inches
HCB plate 93   AKS colour plate XLII

B15 Portrait model of a SHORTHORN BULL in obsidian set with cabochon ruby eyes.
Length 4¼ inches
HCB plate 94

B16 Blue-grey chalcedony WATER BUFFALO with ivory horns and cabochon ruby eyes.
Length 3 inches
HCB plate 86   AKS plate 272

B17 Bowenite BULL, with cabochon ruby eyes in gold settings, shown tossing his head.
Length 2⅝ inches

B18 Pale grey-brown chalcedony BULL with cabochon ruby eyes, shown lowering his head.
Length 2⅜ inches

B14

B19 Dark brown to blue-grey chalcedony MOUNTAIN SHEEP with rose diamond eyes, shown seated. [14]
Length 2⅞ inches

B20 Obsidian white-bearded GNU with rose diamond eyes.
Length 2½ inches

B21 Honey-coloured chalcedony AMERICAN BISON with rose diamond eyes. [15]
Length 2 5/16 inches

B22 Pale brown chalcedony WARTHOG with rose diamond eyes. [15]
Length 2⅝ inches

B23 Small translucent brown chalcedony DONKEY with rose diamond eyes. [14]
Length 1½ inches

B24 GUINEA PIG in cornelian of a pink to straw colour, with cabochon ruby eyes.
Length 2 7/16 inches

B25 Blue-grey to brown chalcedony DORMOUSE with cabochon sapphire eyes, platinum whiskers, shown nibbling gold blades of straw. [15]
Height 2½ inches
HCB plate 86   AKS colour plate XLII

B26 Translucent brown agate MOUSE with rose diamond eyes; ears and tail set in silver.
Length 1⅝ inches
AKS plate 240

B27 White translucent quartzite GUINEA-PIG inlaid with pale patches of tawny aventurine-quartz, ears in cat's-eye quartz and set with cabochon sapphire eyes.
Height 1½ inches
AKS plate 252

B28 Translucent pale blue chalcedony MOUSE with rose diamond eyes; ears and tail set in silver. [14]
Length 1¼ inches

B29 Dark grey chalcedony RAT with rose diamond eyes in gold settings.
Length 1⅜ inches
AKS plate 240

B30 Grey agate RAT with rose diamond eyes; ears and tail set in silver. [14]
Length 1 15/16 inches

B31 White opal RAT with cabochon ruby eyes. [14]
Length 1 inch
AKS plate 240

CASE C

Animal carvings from the collection at Sandringham lent by gracious permission of Her Majesty The Queen.

C1 Brown, mauve and blue chalcedony CHIMPANZEE with olivine eyes, looking deeply troubled. [15]
Height 3 inches
HCB plate 73   AKS plate 240

C2 Obsidian SACRED BABOON with rose diamond eyes. [15]
Height 2¼ inches
HCB plate 87

C3 CHIMPANZEE with folded arms, in varicoloured agate, with olivine eyes. A one-piece carving in which the body is of a tawny colour and the face grey-blue. [15]
Height 2 inches
HCB plate 87

C4 Grey-brown agate CHIMPANZEE, a stylized model set with rose diamond eyes.
Height 1⅜ inches

C5 A pair of amorous MACAQUES clasping each other, carved from a single piece of pale translucent blue-grey chalcedony and set with rose diamond eyes. [16]
Height 1¾ inches

C6 Dark smoky crystal-quartz standing MACAQUE, with rose diamond eyes. A study on the theme 'hear no evil'. [16]
Height 1½ inches

Underside view of C5

C7 Smoky crystal-quartz stump-tailed MACAQUE symbolizing 'see no evil' with its hands covering its eyes. [15]
Length 2¼ inches

C8 RHESUS MONKEY, pausing on all fours, in sandy brown and pale sepia translucent agate, with rose diamond eyes. [15]
Length 2 1/16 inches

C9 Mustard and dark brown crocidolite WILD CAT set with rose diamond eyes; a beast from mythology and carved in the manner of a netsuke, with ferocious expression and sharp teeth.
Length 1 9/16 inches

C10 Coiled SNAKE, carved from one piece of brown and black jasper perfectly describing the natural marking and set with rose diamond eyes. This object is taken directly from a carved wood netsuke now in the Bauer Collection, Geneva.

C9

C11 SNAKE in brown and black speckled jasper set with pale olivine eyes and gold fangs, carved as a rising coil through which the head emerges, mouth open to hiss. Presumably this is also taken from a netsuke. [15]
Height 1½ inches

C12 Seated AFRICAN ELEPHANT of grey brown chalcedony with rose diamond eyes. [16]
Height 1 7/16 inches

C13 Bowenite INDIAN ELEPHANT, with cabochon sapphire eyes, its trunk extended.
Length 1½ inches

C14 Siberian nephrite standing INDIAN ELEPHANT with brilliant diamond eyes set in gold.
Length 4 9/16 inches

C15 Purpurine stylized carving of an INDIAN ELEPHANT of almost globular form, with rose diamond eyes. [16]
Length 1¾ inches

C16 Nephrite carving of an ELEPHANT with rose diamond eyes in gold settings.
Length 1 5/16 inches

C17 A twin to the previous exhibit.

C18 INDIAN ELEPHANT PENDANT, of grey-white chalcedony, set with cabochon ruby eyes, shown with trunk raised. With a band of engraved red and yellow golds set with two rose diamonds, with suspension ring attached.
Length 1 1/16 inches

C19 Carrot-coloured sardonyx ELEPHANT with rose diamond eyes. It bears on its back a gold tower enamelled with opaque white bricks and set with rose diamonds; a yellow gold rug underneath enamelled translucent emerald over a *guilloché* field has fringes set with rose diamonds. Probably intended as a reference to the Royal Danish Elephant.
Height 1 inch

C20 Rock crystal ELEPHANT with cabochon ruby eyes, bearing on its back a red gold rug on which sits a yellow and red gold tower enamelled with translucent rust-coloured bricks and set with rose diamonds. This model also recalls the Royal Danish Elephant.
Height 1 inch

C21 Gun-metal automaton INDIAN ELEPHANT with cabochon ruby eyes and ivory tusks; an opaque white enamelled *mahout* (elephant tender) carrying an elephant-hook sits on a rose diamond-set yellow gold rug enamelled translucent green and opaque white. One of the diamond collets may be moved aside and a gold key inserted to wind the clockwork mechanism; when a tiny lever under the stomach is pressed, the elephant walks slowly along swinging its head and tail. This toy was given by his family to HM King George V on Christmas Day 1929.
Length 1 7/8 inches   No marks
AKS colour plate XXX

C20   C21   C19

C22 HIPPOPOTAMUS in striated grey-brown chalcedony with rose diamond eyes.
Length $2\frac{5}{16}$ inches

C23 Obsidian carving of a stylized seated HIPPOPOTAMUS with rose diamond eyes.
Length $2\frac{3}{16}$ inches

C24 Pale grey chalcedony carving of a HIPPOPOTAMUS with its mouth open, set with cabochon ruby eyes.
Length $2\frac{3}{16}$ inches

C25 Nephrite carving of a fat HIPPOPOTAMUS with rose diamond eyes.
Length $2\frac{5}{16}$ inches

C26 Bowenite HIPPOPOTAMUS with a melancholy expression, set with pale cabochon sapphire eyes.
Length $1\frac{7}{16}$ inches

C22
C25   C24   C23
                          C26

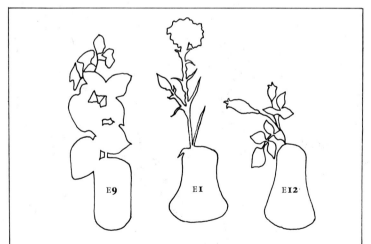

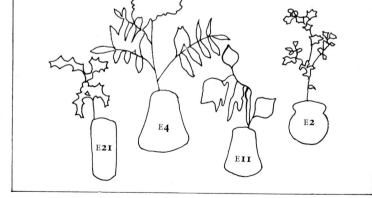

c27 Honey-coloured agate KOALA with cabochon emerald eyes, poised on a chased silver branch. [15]
Length of koala 2 13/16 inches   Signed HW

c28 Nephrite BEAVER on its haunches, with rose diamond eyes set in gold. [15]
Height 2 3/16 inches

c29 Californian SEA LION in obsidian with rose diamond eyes, on a rock crystal ice floe. [15]
Length of sea lion 3 1/16 inches

c30 Pale sea-green bowenite BROWN BEAR with cabochon ruby eyes set in gold. [16]
Length 2 inches
AKS plate 272

c31 Agate BROWN BEAR set with rose diamond eyes. [15]
Length 1 9/16 inches

c32 AARDVARK in banded agate in shades of brown, blue, ochre and grey, with rose diamond eyes. [15]
Length 2 5/8 inches   HCB plate 87

c33 BACTRIAN CAMEL in bowenite, set with cabochon ruby eyes. [16]
Length 2 1/2 inches

c34 Nephrite CHAMELEON with brilliant diamond eyes set in gold.
Length 2 5/16 inches   AKS plate 273

c35 Pale brown chalcedony DUCK-BILLED PLATYPUS with rose diamond eyes. [15]
Length 2 13/16 inches   AKS plate 227

c36 Spinach jade KANGAROO with baby in her pouch, both with rose diamond eyes.
Height 3 3/8 inches
HCB plate 87

c36

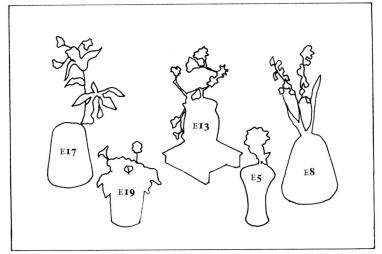

OVERLEAF ▲

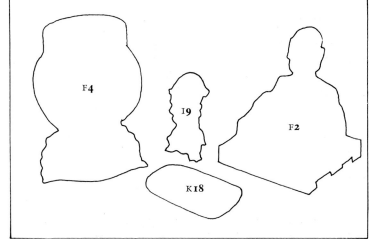

OPPOSITE ▲

CASE D

Carvings of birds from the collection at Sandringham lent by gracious permission of Her Majesty The Queen.

D1 MARIBOU STORK in vari-coloured grey-brown agate, with rose diamond eyes and chased gold legs. [29]
Height 3⅝ inches   Signed HW

D2 Grey-blue chalcedony MARIBOU STORK with rose diamond eyes and chased gold legs.
Height 3½ inches   Gold mark 72   Signed HW

D3 Rock crystal model of the GREAT AUK, satin finished, with cabochon ruby eyes set in silver. [29]
Height 2¾ inches
AKS plate 230

D4 COCKATOO in multi-coloured agate with shades of yellow, chestnut, and rust, with rose diamond eyes and chased gold claws, on a swinging gold perch fitted with two feeding bowls. [29]
Height 5 inches   Perch signed МΠ

D5 Vari-coloured grey chalcedony PENGUIN with rose diamond eyes and chased red gold feet. [29]
Height 2⅛ inches   Gold mark 72   Signed HW
AKS plate 230

D6 Standing GOOSE in white quartzite with obsidian head and inlaid labradorite feathers, beak in stained quartzite, rose diamond eyes and chased red gold legs.
Length 2¼ inches   Gold mark 72   Signed HW

D7 Another GOOSE of the same materials as the previous exhibit, but with outstretched neck.
Length 2⅞ inches   Gold mark 72   Signed HW
AKS colour plate XLII

D8 Pale grey-brown chalcedony CHICK with cabochon ruby eyes and gold legs.
Height 1 7/16 inches

D9 Agate CHICK in tones of mauve, brown and black, set with olivine eyes, with chased gold legs.
Length 1⅜ inches

D10 Honey-coloured agate CHICK with rose diamond eyes and chased gold legs.
Height 1 5/16 inches

D11 Swimming SWAN of creamy chalcedony with cabochon ruby eyes.
Length 2 inches
AKS plate 227

D12 Pale cream chalcedony SWAN with cabochon ruby eyes, delving among its feathers.
Length 1½ inches

D13 Vari-coloured agate ROBIN with cabochon ruby eyes and chased gold legs. The patch on the breast is vividly expressed in the stone. [29]
Length 1 15/16 inches

D14 Pale pinky-white chalcedony HEN with cabochon ruby eyes and chased red gold legs.
Length 1 inch
AKS plate 230

D15 Reddish brown agate HEN with rose diamond eyes and chased gold legs.
Length ⅞ inch

D16 Pinky-brown to grey-blue chalcedony COCK PHEASANT with rose diamond eyes and chased gold legs. [29]
Length 2½ inches

D17 Crocidolite JUNGLE FOWL with rose diamond eyes and chased red gold legs. [29]
Length 2⅞ inches   Signed HW
AKS colour plate XLII

D18 PIGEON carved from a piece of grey and black moss-agate, with cabochon ruby eyes. [29]
Length 1⅛ inches

D19 COCKATOO in crocidolite, with rose diamond eyes and chased gold claws, perched in a

silver-gilt cage which opens and is fitted with two feeding bowls and a removable drawer.
Height 4⅛ inches   Cage signed MΠ

D20 A pair of nephrite BUDGERIGARS, with rose diamond eyes and gold claws, on a chased silver-gilt swinging perch, with two feeding-bowls set with rose diamonds and enamelled pale translucent green and opalescent white over *guilloché* surfaces.
Height 6⅝ inches   Perch signed MΠ

D21 Obsidian TURKEY with lapis lazuli head, purpurine comb, rose diamond eyes and chased pink gold feet. [29]
Height 3¹³⁄₁₆ inches   Signed HW
HCB plate 95   AKS plate 273

D22 Chalcedony GOOSE in tones of grey, with cabochon ruby eyes and chased greeny-yellow gold legs.
Height 4¹⁄₁₆ inches
AKS plate 252

D23 Grey-brown chalcedony DUCKLING with cabochon ruby eyes and red gold legs.
Height 1⅜ inches

D24 Cornelian DUCKLING of mustard colour, with cabochon ruby eyes and chased red gold legs.
Height 1⁵⁄₁₆ inches   Gold mark 72   Signed HW
AKS colour plate XLII

D25 Pale butter-coloured chalcedony DUCK-LING, with olivine eyes and chased red gold legs.
Height 2¾ inches   Signed HW

D26 Pale creamy-brown DUCKLING in chalcedony, with cabochon ruby eyes and chased red gold legs.
Height 1⅞ inches   Gold mark 72   Signed HW

D27 Pale creamy-brown quartzite DUCKLING flapping its wings, with rose diamond eyes foiled pale green, chased red gold legs.
Height 2¼ inches   Gold mark 72   Signed HW
AKS colour plate XLII

D28 Vari-coloured grey to mauve agate DUCK, carved to simulate a downy texture, with rose diamond eyes and chased yellow gold legs.
Height 1⅛ inches
AKS colour plate XLII

D29 Bowenite CHICK with cabochon ruby eyes and chased gold legs. This chick is carved in a manner that recalls the paintings of Bosch. [29]
Height 1⁵⁄₁₆ inches   Gold mark 72   Signed HW

D30 Rhodonite BABY BIRD designed in the form of an egg, with olivine eyes. [29]
Height ¹⁵⁄₁₆ inch

D31 Bowenite carving of a DODO, set with ruby eyes. [29]
Length 1⅞ inches

D32 Pale grey chalcedony GULL, with cabochon ruby eyes.
Length 2 inches

D33 One piece carving of a HORNBILL, in chalcedony of pale and dark grey, with rose diamond eyes and gold claws, perched in a silver-gilt cage which opens and has a drawer and two feeding bowls. [30]
Height of cage 3⅝ inches   Signed MΠ
AKS plate 238

D34 Obsidian COCKEREL with purpurine comb, jasper wattles, rose diamond eyes and chased pink gold feet. [29]
Height 3⅞ inches   Signed HW
HCB plate 95   AKS plate 273

D35 Mauve, pink and white agate HEN, with rose diamond eyes and chased red gold legs. [29]
Height 2¼ inches   Gold mark 72   Signed HW

D36 Honey-coloured chalcedony COCKEREL, with rose diamond eyes and gold legs.
Height 1¹³⁄₁₆ inches

D37 Stylized carving of a YOUNG RAVEN in nephrite with rose diamond eyes. [29]
Height 1⅝ inches

D38 An OWL in carrot-coloured agate, with rose diamond eyes. This tiny sculpture is full of character despite its size and looks unmistakably ruffled and flustered. [16]
Height ⅝ inch

D39 Honey-coloured agate COCKATOO, with olivine eyes and gold claws, chained to a pendant silver-gilt perch with two feeding bowls. The supporting pole is enamelled translucent green.
Height 5¼ inches   Signed MΠ

D40 Pale green-grey chalcedony domesticated PIGEON, probably of a variety known as Turbit, with cabochon ruby eyes and chased gold legs. [29]
Length 2 inches

D41 Brown agate POUTER-PIGEON with rose diamond eyes and chased gold legs.
Length 1⅝ inches

D42 Translucent blue-grey DUCK, with cabochon ruby eyes and chased gold legs.
Length 1 11/16 inches

D43 Aventurine-quartz SPARROW, with rose diamond eyes in silver mounts. This conventionalized model is based on Fabergé's admiration for Japanese netsuke. See also D44 and D45.
Length 1½ inches

D44 Pale bowenite pecking SPARROW, with cabochon ruby eyes.
Length 1½ inches

D45 Nephrite SPARROW with rose diamond eyes.
Length 1½ inches
AKS plate 248

D46 Pinky-brown agate FLAMINGO with rose diamond eyes and chased dull red gold legs. [29]
Height 4 inches   Signed HW

D47 Vari-coloured agate KIWI, with rose diamond eyes and chased yellow gold legs and beak. [29]
Height 2 inches   Gold mark 72   Signed HW

D48 FANTAIL DOVE in grey-brown banded agate, with rose diamond eyes and chased gold legs.
Height 1 7/8 inches

D49 MANDARIN DUCK carved from striated blue-grey banded agate, with cabochon ruby eyes and chased gold legs.
Length 2 7/16 inches

D50 Grey vari-coloured chalcedony OSTRICH, with rose diamond eyes and chased red gold legs. [29]
Height 3 5/16 inches
AKS plate 240

D51 HAMMERKOP in brown agate, with rose diamond eyes and chased yellow gold legs. [29]
Height 3¼ inches   Gold mark 72   Signed HW

D52 KINGFISHER in bowenite with cabochon ruby eyes. This and the following sculpture are good examples of Fabergé's humorous treatment of his subject. [29]
Height 2 1/16 inches

D53 KINGFISHER in dark Siberian nephrite, with rose diamond eyes and chased gold claws. [29]
Height 2 5/16 inches   Gold mark 72
Signed HW

D54 Pale coffee-coloured quartzite PELICAN, with olivine eyes.
Height 2½ inches
AKS plate 227

D55 MAGPIE with translucent white quartzite body and labradorite head, feathers with blue tones, rose diamond eyes and gold legs.
Length 2 inches
AKS colour plate XLII

D56 SWALLOW in obsidian and inlaid white quartzite, with rose diamond eyes and chased gold legs.
Length 2 5/8 inches
AKS plate 230

D57 Black and brown flecked jasper OWL, with rose diamond eyes and red gold claws, on a chased green gold perch supported on white onyx base. [30]
Height 1 11/16 inches   Gold mark 72
Perch signed HW

D58 Obsidian VULTURE, with translucent brown sardonyx head, rose diamond eyes and chased red gold legs on a red gilt engraved silver perch. [30]
Height 1 7/8 inches   Signed МП
AKS plate 272

D59 Stylized RAVEN of dark grey and brown striated agate, with gold feet and rose diamond eyes, on an oxidised silver perch supported on white onyx base. [30]
Height 2 inches
AKS plate 230

CASE E

Flower studies from the collection at Sandringham lent by gracious permission of Her Majesty The Queen.

E1 CARNATION in yellow gold enamelled translucent red-bronze, the engraved green gold stalk, leaves and bud washed with translucent green enamel, in a rock crystal pot. [39]
Height $7\frac{1}{4}$ inches   No marks
AKS plate 299

E2 JAPONICA, the blossom in pinky white opaque enamel with rose-diamond centres, engraved dull green gold stalk, carved nephrite leaves, in a rock crystal pot. [40]
Height $6\frac{3}{4}$ inches   No marks
AKS plate 300

E3 CONVOLVULUS in gold, growing in a bowenite trough, with two pale blue and two pink enamelled flowers with rose diamond centres, carved jade leaves; climbing up an opalescent oyster-enamelled pole set in simulated soil of gold. [62]
Height $4\frac{1}{2}$ inches   No marks
HCB plate 78

E4 ROWAN TREE, with purpurine berries, dull red gold stem and pale carved nephrite leaves, in a rock crystal vase. [40]
Height 9 inches   No marks
HCB plate 84   AKS plate 293

E5 Yellow gold ROSE AND BUD enamelled opaque pink, with green translucent enamelled leaves and rose diamond dew-drop, in a rock crystal vase. [41]
Height $3\frac{7}{16}$ inches   No marks
AKS plate 303

E6 BLEEDING-HEART in rhodonite and white chalcedony, dull green gold stalks, carved nephrite leaves, in a rock crystal vase. [cover]
Height $7\frac{3}{4}$ inches   No marks
HCB plate 85   AKS plate 294

E7 CHRYSANTHEMUM of green gold thinly enamelled pale yellow and pink, with carved nephrite leaves, in a square rock crystal vase.
Height $9\frac{7}{8}$ inches   Signed HW
HCB plate 85   AKS plate 303

E8 LILIES OF THE VALLEY in pearls and rose diamonds, on green gold stalk with carved nephrite leaves, in a rock crystal jar. [41]
Height $5\frac{7}{16}$ inches   No marks
AKS plate 303

E9 RASPBERRY, with four berries carved in rhodonite and two unripe ones in jade; stalk of gold and leaves carved in nephrite, in a cylindrical rock crystal pot. [39]
Height $6\frac{3}{8}$ inches   No marks
HCB plate 83   AKS colour plate XXX

E10 SMALL RASPBERRY PLANT in carved rhodonite with nephrite leaves and red gold stalk, in a rock crystal jar.
Height $3\frac{9}{16}$ inches   No marks
AKS plate 302

E11 CATKINS in spun green gold, stalk in dull red gold and leaves carved in nephrite. [40]
Height $5\frac{7}{8}$ inches   No marks
AKS plate 293

E12 ROSEBUDS enamelled opaque pink and translucent green, stalk in red gold, leaves carved in nephrite, in a rock crystal pot. [39]
Height $5\frac{1}{2}$ inches   No marks
HCB plate 83   AKS plate 294

E13 PINE TREE in engraved dull red gold set with rose diamonds, in a carved bowenite vase supported on aventurine quartz platform. This model was taken from nature at Sandringham. [41]
Height $5\frac{1}{8}$ inches   No marks
HCB plate 83   AKS plate 292

E14 PANSY enamelled opaque violet with brilliant diamond centre, nephrite leaves, green gold stalk, in a rock crystal pot.
Height 6 inches   No marks
AKS plate 302

E15 SMALL PANSY enamelled opaque violet with naturalistic markings and a brilliant diamond centre, gold stalk and jade leaves, in a rock crystal pot.
Height $4\frac{1}{4}$ inches   No marks
AKS plate 301

E16 MOCK-ORANGE in white quartzite with olivine centres, on a red gold stalk with carved nephrite leaves, in a rock crystal jar.
Height $5\frac{9}{16}$ inches   No marks
HCB plate 83   AKS plate 303

E17 WILD CHERRIES in carved purpurine, blossom enamelled opaque white with brilliant diamond centres, the two stalks in dull red gold, leaves carved in nephrite, in a rock crystal pot. [41]
Height $5\frac{3}{8}$ inches   No marks
HCB plate 82   AKS plate 293

E18 Pink and white opaque enamelled WILD ROSE, with red gold stamens and set with a brilliant diamond centre, with green gold stalk and nephrite leaves, in a rock crystal jar.
Height $5\frac{3}{4}$ inches   No marks
AKS plate 301

E19 FIVE FIELD DAISIES, each flowerhead enamelled opaque white, pale pink and translucent pale green behind, with bronze-foiled rose diamond centres, on green gold stalks, nephrite leaves, in a silver flower-pot enamelled opaque terracotta with simulated soil within. [41]
Height $3\frac{1}{16}$ inches   Signed HW
AKS plate 301

E20 FLOWERING CRANBERRY, with carved cornelian and chalcedony berries, nephrite leaves, red gold stalk, in a rock crystal vase.
Height $4\frac{5}{8}$ inches   No marks
AKS plate 302

E21 HOLLY, with berries carved in purpurine, stalk in dull green gold, the leaves of highly polished dark nephrite to express their naturalistic glossy surface, in a cylindrical rock crystal pot. [40]
Height $5\frac{7}{8}$ inches   No marks
HCB plate 82   AKS plate 292

CASE F

Objects lent by gracious permission of Her Majesty The Queen and H.M. The Queen Mother, and the Victoria and Albert Museum.

F1 EASTER EGG enamelled pale tranclusent pink and opaque white on a yellow gold *guilloché* surface with twelve reserve panels. Each panel with a painted enamel motif in pale violet and divided by broad bands of opaque enamelled Indian red roses and translucent green enamel leaves on a dull granulated gold field, and set with rose diamonds. The initials of Barbara Kelch appear under a portrait diamond set in the top; the year of its presentation, 1899, under another portrait in the base. The surprise, that was once inside, has been lost.

Barbara Kelch was a wealthy eccentric woman whose doting husband, Alexander Ferdinandovitch Kelch, presented her with Easter eggs quite on a par with those given by the Tsar. (There are four known examples.) [52]
Height 3½ inches   No gold marks
Signed МП
AKS colour plate LXXXIII
From Queen Mary's collection.

F2 Rose quartz carving of a MAGOT, with head in dark blue-grey agate and hands in brown agate, seated with crossed legs, on a massive green fluor-spar stand. He wears a gold belt enamelled opalescent oyster set with cabochon rubies and rose diamonds, earrings in rose diamonds, and has cabochon ruby eyes. The head, hands and carved ruby tongue are delicately balanced so that the slightest movement sets them in motion. [42]
Height 6¼ inches   No marks
HCB plate 72
From Queen Mary's collection.

F3 COLONNADE EGG, presented to Alexandra Feodorovna by Nicholas II, probable date, 1905.

Conceived as an arcadian Temple of Love, this rotary clock Egg commemorates the birth of the long-awaited heir to the throne in 1904. A silver-gilt cupid, an allegorical representation of the Tsarevitch, surmounts the gold Egg, which is enamelled opalescent pale pink on an engraved ground and is encircled by the broad band of a translucent white enamelled dial set with rose diamond numerals; a diamond-set pointer projects from a colonnade in pale green bowenite, which supports the Egg. The base of this colonnade, which is made up of six gold-mounted Ionic columns, is set with coloured gold chiselled mounts and a broad band of pale pink enamel. Four silver-gilt cherubs, representing the Tsar's four daughters, are seated at intervals around this elaborate base and are linked by floral swags chiselled in *quatre-couleur* gold. Two cast and chased platinum doves are perched on a white enamel plinth raised within the circle of columns.

Sir Sacheverell Sitwell has suggested that the design for this Egg derives from Eisen's illustrations to *Les Baisers* of Dorat. (See *Carl Fabergé*, Wartski Coronation Exhibition 1953.) [51]
Height 11¼ inches   Signed HW
HCB plate 61   AKS colour plate LXXVII
From Queen Mary's collection.

F4 ROCK CRYSTAL VASE of bellied form engraved with the Royal Arms and the date 1911 of the Coronation of George V and Queen Mary 'June XXII, MCMXI'.

Mounted in granulated gold decorated with multi-coloured opaque and translucent enamels, it is set with cabochon rubies, emeralds and sapphires and is supported on three claw feet. The gift of Leopold de Rothschild, this vase arrived at Buckingham Palace for the Coronation breakfast table, filled with the most beautiful orchids from the Rothschilds' house at Gunnersbury. [42]
Height 6½ inches   Gold mark 72   Signed МП
HCB plate 70*

F5 MOSAIC EGG, presented to Alexandra Feodorovna by Nicholas II. Dated 1914. An Easter egg, the skeleton of which consists of a system of yellow gold belts to which is applied a platinum network partially *pavé* set with diamonds and coloured gems including sapphires, rubies, emeralds, topaz quartz and green demantoid garnets in flower patterns.

The Egg is divided into five oval panels by these gold belts which are set with half pearls within lines of opaque white enamel and five brilliant diamonds are set at each intersection; it is further decorated by grilles of rose diamond scrolls and the rounder end is set with a moonstone beneath which may be seen the gold initials of the Tsarina in Russian characters inlaid in an opaque pale pink enamelled plaque serving as a foil.

The surprise concealed inside, and held in place by two gold clips, consists of a gold, pearl and translucent green and opaque white enamelled pedestal set with diamonds and green garnets and supporting an oval plaque surmounted by a diamond Imperial Crown. On one side of the plaque is painted, in pale sepia *grisaille* enamel, the profiles of the five Imperial children against a background of engraved vertical parallel lines enamelled opalescent *rose Pompadour*. The reverse is enamelled with a pale sepia basket of flowers against a pale green background, around which the year 1914 and the names of the children are written in sepia on the opaque ivory enamelled border. Designed as a jewel, this beautiful Egg was made in Holmström's workshop and is engraved with the name К. ФАБЕРЖЕ, but underneath the pedestal, in addition to the sun-in-splendour design, the words G. Fabergé, 1914 have been engraved, presumably by a later misguided hand. [52]
Height of Egg 3⅝ inches
Height of pedestal 3 inches
HCB plate 51 and colour plate 52
AKS colour plates LXXIX and LXXX
From Queen Mary's collection.

F6 MINIATURE LOUIS XV ROLL-TOP DESK, in chased yellow and red golds enamelled translucent pale mauve and opalescent white; the interior is lined with engraved mother-of-pearl and divided into pigeon holes. A small gold key locks this perfect miniature.
Height 4⅜ inches   Signed HW
AKS plate 285

F7 Gold-mounted silver PRESENTATION BOX' enamelled translucent pale mauve over an engraved ground in imitation of watered silk, the hinged cover decorated with four diamond-set Romanov double-headed Eagles and a diamond-framed miniature painting of Nicholas II signed by Rockstuhl. The borders are chased with dull green gold laurel leaves and the box is embellished with pink gold mounts and rosettes.
Length 4 inches   Gold mark 72
Signed HW
HCB plate 110

F8 SPRAY OF GOLD CORNFLOWERS enamelled translucent blue and set with brilliant and rose diamonds, with a freely swinging stem of oats in dull gold, both in a rock crystal vase. [61]
Height 7 15/16 inches   No marks
HCB plate 35   AKS plate 285

F9 SPRAY OF BUTTERCUPS in gold enamelled translucent yellow and green over engraved grounds, and cornflowers enamelled translucent blue with diamond centres, with green gold stalks and leaves in a rock crystal jar. A

diamond, ruby and black-enamelled bee in red gold is poised on one of the buttercups. [61]
Height 9 inches   No marks
AKS plate 304

F10 A gold diamond-set PRESENTATION BOX, enamelled translucent yellow over a *guilloché* ground, with chased red and green gold wreaths and borders, the crowned cypher of Nicholas II on the hinged cover.
3¼ inches square   Signed A★H

F6–F10 lent by gracious permission of Her Majesty Queen Elizabeth, The Queen Mother.

F11 Square yellow gold IMPERIAL PRESENTATION BOX, with canted corners, chased red and green gold scrolling and foliate borders, the hinged cover with a large diamond-shaped reserve panel enamelled opalescent oyster and applied with the Imperial Cypher of Nicholas II within a crowned oval frame of brilliant diamonds; the corners of the cover enamelled translucent yellow over sunray engraving are each overlaid with an opaque black-enamelled Romanov double-headed eagle. The sides of the box are enamelled translucent yellow over engine-turning. Given to the Museum, through the National Art Collections Fund, by the late Sir William Seeds, KCMG, former ambassador in Moscow.
3 3/16 inches square   Signed МП
AKS colour plate IV
Victoria and Albert Museum.

OPPOSITE *Above left* K22   *Below left* K24
Right F3

51

CASE G

Objects from the collection at Sandringham lent by gracious permission of Her Majesty The Queen.

G1 Carved Siberian nephrite CIGARETTE CASE, decorated with engraved red gold strapwork mounts, simulating a miniature piece of luggage.
Length 3½ inches   Signed МП

G2 Carved agate scent FLACON, in Chinese taste, set with rose diamonds, with two strawberry-enamelled rings suspended from masks carved on either side; the globular gold-mounted top is also enamelled translucent strawberry over an engraved ground with a moonstone finial.
Height 3 inches   Signed МП

G3 Silver and nephrite WRITING TABLET-CASE, mounted with red gold margins and a chased green gold foliate wreath.
Height 5 inches   Signed КФ

G4 Engraved smoky crystal-quartz SCENT BOTTLE, in the form of a lyre, with red gold mounts and set with rose diamonds, the top enamelled translucent pink and surmounted by a pearl finial.
Height 2-9/16 inches   Signed МП
Gold mark crossed anchors

OPPOSITE *Left and Middle* F5   *Right* F1

G5 Siberian nephrite tall CUP mounted in dull green gold set with rose diamonds, the handle inset with a rouble of 1756 enamelled translucent strawberry colour.
Height 2⅞ inches
Signed ФАБЕРЖЕ but maker's mark indecipherable

G6 Silver GUM POT of onion form enamelled opalescent oyster over an engraved ground with red gold mounts, the brush-holder with a chased foliate motif surmounted by a cabochon amethyst finial. Fabergé made many gum pots of similar design and, although this example does not bear his mark, but marks of the 3rd co-operative or *Artel*, it is included in the exhibition as probable evidence of Fabergé's workmen participating, as it is known they did, in this interesting early exercise in workers' initiative.
Width 1¾ inches   Signed ЗяА
See note and illustration of mark, AKS page 119

G7 Hinged nephrite JAR mounted in red gold, with chased green gold laurel border, the clasp set with rose diamonds and two cabochon rubies.
Diameter 1⅝ inches
Signed ФАБЕРЖЕ, maker's mark indecipherable

G8 Simple red gold STRUT CLOCK enamelled opalescent oyster over an engraved ground.
2-7/16 inches square   Signed HW

G9 Hanging BELL-PUSH of globular form in nephrite with red and dull green gold chased mounts and a moonstone push-piece.
Height 2 inches   Unsigned

G10 Silver TABLE-BELL with an engraved yellow gold handle, enamelled opalescent oyster, decorated with chased red and green gold swags and bows, and surmounted by a cabochon ruby.
Height 3¼ inches   Signed К. ФАБЕРЖЕ
AKS plate 161

G11 Siberian jade double-opening CIGARETTE CASE mounted in red gold with chased green gold laurel borders and with a brilliant diamond push-piece.
Length 3⅛ inches   Gold mark crossed anchors
Signed МП

G12 Small HAND SEAL in red and green golds, enamelled opaque white with translucent emerald leaves and strawberry pellets, surmounted by a white onyx ball and set with an engraved cornelian for sealing.
Height 1-15/16 inches   Signed МП
AKS plate 146

G13 Nephrite JAR AND COVER carved as a pear, with red gold mounts, the finial in green gold is designed as a spray of leaves set with rose diamonds culminating in an engraved stalk. [62]
Height 1⅞ inches   Signed МП
AKS plate 188

G14 Small HAND SEAL in yellow gold, the waisted stem, enamelled opaque white, supports a nephrite egg carved with spiral flutes; the sealing stone is of agate.
Height 1⅞ inches   Signed МП

G15 Rectangular STAMP-BOX in nephrite opening at the top by means of two lids meeting diagonally. The hinges are mounted with yellow gold arabesque motifs set with rose diamonds and two cabochon rubies, and the interior of the box divides into three compartments, the floors of which slope gently to enable the stamps to be the more easily removed. [63]
Length 2 15/16 inches   Signed МП

G16 SCENT FLACON enamelled overall in opalescent oyster over a *guilloché* ground, with a red and green gold chased laurel border, the hinged top with a rose diamond and cabochon ruby cluster finial.
Height 1 13/16 inches   Signed МП

G17 Siberian jade GUM POT in the form of an egg, with a chased red gold sunburst mount and a brush-holder with dull green gold chased leaves topped by a moonstone finial.
Length 1¾ inches   Signed МП

G18 White onyx BELL-PUSH decorated with chased red gold mounts supported on four ball feet. The push a small nephrite carving of a frog with rose diamond eyes, crouching on a yellow gold rug enamelled opaque white with black dots and opalescent red beads.
Length 2 1/16 inches   Signed МП
AKS plate 188

G19 Siberian jade BOX formed as an egg, with *fleur-de-lis* clasp and hinge as a crown in yellow gold set with six cabochon rubies and rose diamonds in silver.
Length 1¾ inches   No marks

G20 Hinged nephrite BOX designed in the shape of a segment of cheese, mounted in yellow gold and set with *fleur-de-lis* motifs in rose diamonds, that on the cover with an elongated oval cabochon ruby. [63]
Length 1 7/16 inches   Signed МП
AKS plate 128

CASE H

Objects from the collection at Sandringham lent by gracious permission of Her Majesty The Queen.

H1 Rectangular nephrite BOX, mounted in red gold with chased green gold laurel borders; the hinged cover is inset with a gold panel with an enamelled painting in sepia against an opalescent pale pink background of the Houses of Parliament.
Length 5¼ inches   Signed HW
HCB plate 90

H2 PORTRAIT BUST OF TSAR ALEXANDER III, carved in a transparent gold-coloured crystal quartz supported upon a Siberian jade column rising from a square base. A chased yellow and red gold Romanov double-headed eagle is applied to the front of the column.
Height 6 15/16 inches   No marks

H3 Rectangular nephrite STRUT FRAME, mounted in red gold with a border of half-pearls, containing a gold panel with a view of Sandringham House, painted in warm sepia over a pale opalescent rose background.
Length 5 15/16 inches   Signed HW

H4 Octagonal nephrite BOX, with yellow gold chased mounts enriched with opalescent enamelled beads surrounding the rose-sepia enamelled painting on gold of a riverside church.
Width 2⅝ inches   Signed HW
AKS plate 188

H5 Rectangular nephrite BOX, mounted in red gold with a chased green gold foliate border with, on the hinged cover, an opalescent sepia enamel painting framed with half-pearls of a lakeside view of Sandringham House.
Length 4 inches   Signed HW
HCB plate 88

H6 Circular nephrite BOX, mounted in red gold and green gold chased with laurel, the hinged cover inset with a gold panel bordered by half-pearls, enamel-painted with a broad avenue of trees in sepia over an opalescent background.
Diameter 2½ inches   Signed HW

H7 A red gold rectangular STRUT FRAME, enamelled translucent emerald green over an engraved ground with, at intervals, white opaque enamelled ties. It contains an opalescent rose-sepia enamelled painting on gold of the Dairy at Sandringham where the wax models for the Sandringham animals were assembled for the inspection of the King and Queen.
Length 2 13/16 inches   Signed HW
HCB plate 89

H8 BONBONNIÈRE in engraved yellow gold, of circular *bombé* form, the box and cover enamelled with wreathed paintings of Balmoral and Windsor Castles respectively, in warm sepia against opalescent backgrounds. Both paintings are bordered by opaque white-enamelled pellets and the box is encircled by an elaborate frieze composed of painted enamel roses and translucent green leaves with rose diamonds.
Diameter 2¼ inches   Gold mark 72
Signed HW   HCB plate 91   AKS plate 91

H9 Circular BOX, in engraved yellow gold enamelled overall pale opalescent white and sepia, decorated with opaque white enamelled pellets and with naturalistically coloured borders of leaves and berries in translucent enamel. The hinged cover depicts Falconet's Peter the Great monument in St Petersburg, within a wreath, the bottom with a view of the Peter and Paul Fortress, all enamel painted. Around the side of the box are painted loosely entwined foliate trails in panels.
Diameter 2 9/16 inches   Gold mark 72
Signed HW   AKS colour plate XXX

H10 Square silver BOX with canted corners, with red and chased green gold laurel borders and a rose diamond thumb-piece. Sides and base enamelled translucent grey-blue, the hinged lid with a sepia enamel painting of the Peter the Great monument over an opalescent background. [63]
1½ inches square   Signed ΦA

Above H3
Middle: left to right H8, H7, H8
Below H5

CASE I

Objects from the collection at Sandringham lent by gracious permission of Her Majesty The Queen.

11 WINE GLASS with red gold sunray fluted base and green gold chased laurel border, the trumpet-shaped stem enamelled opalescent pink over a *guilloché* ground with single sprigs of green gold reserved leaves. The bowl is of carved rock crystal.
Height 3 inches   Signed MП

12 TABLE CLOCK in rock crystal engraved with trophies, the opaque white-enamelled dial framed by a red gold border chased with leaves enamelled translucent emerald with rose diamond ties. The four lobes of the clock are divided by gold arrows with rose diamond bow-knots set with cabochon ruby centres. The hands are of engraved and pierced red gold and the curved strut is of reeded silver. The clock, which was given by Alexandra Feodorovna to Queen Victoria, had its permanent place on the desk of George V.
Height and width 4 $\frac{15}{16}$ inches   Signed MП
AKS plate 146

13 Red gold and rock crystal covered EGG CUP, the trumpet-shaped stem embossed with concentric circles. The cover of the oviform container is mounted with a carved moonstone finial modelled as a helmeted female head, possibly that of Minerva, rising from a collar

of alternating rose diamonds and cabochon rubies. Within, the gold base is enamelled *champlevé* in translucent deep red with the monogram composed of the letters X.B. for *Christos voskress*, – Christ is risen. This container, which resembles a pyx, was presumably intended for the traditional egg to be presented on Easter morning.
Height 4 $\frac{3}{8}$ inches   Gold mark crossed anchors
Signed EK

14 TABLE CLOCK of hoof form, on bun feet, in carved bowenite, mounted in red-gilt silver with red and green gold foliate swags. The plain white-enamelled dial, fitted with pierced red gold hands, is bordered by half-pearls set in red gold and is surmounted by a rose diamond bow.
Diameter without feet 3 $\frac{7}{8}$ inches   Signed MП

15 Rectangular carved bowenite FRAME chased with a red and green gold acanthus border with a red gold strut and ivory back. It holds a painting of Durham Cathedral in translucent warm sepia enamel over an engraved gold background.
Length 6 $\frac{3}{16}$ inches   Signed HW
HCB plate 90   AKS plate 91

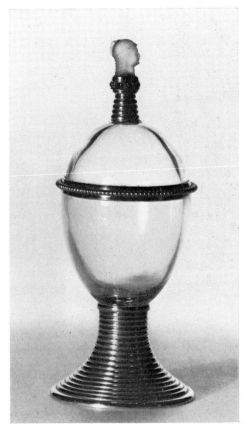

16 Shallow circular KOVSH (scoop or ladle) carved in bowenite, supported on a dull yellow gold fluted base; the gold handle, mounted with a single pearl, is inset with a Catherine the Great rouble dated 1766 enamelled translucent strawberry colour and bordered by rose diamonds.
Overall length 4⅜ inches   Signed EK
Gold mark crossed anchors
HCB plate 101

17 Rock crystal BOX in the form of an egg, with red and green gold *repoussé* clasp and hinge in rococo taste set with rose diamonds.
[63]
Length 2 3/16 inches   Signed МП
AKS plate 188

18 HAND SEAL, the main column in reeded red gold decorated with Greek key and Vitruvian scroll borders and foliate swags in yellow and green golds, the top composed of a heavy block of bowenite carved in triangular form. Set with an agate sealing stone.
Height 2¼ inches   Signed МП
Gold mark crossed anchors

19 Model of a TERRESTRIAL GLOBE, in engraved rock crystal, supported on a dull green silver-gilt stand with burnished red gold chased mounts. This early object illustrates how Kollin was feeling his way towards effects he later achieved with golds of differing shades.
[42]
Height 3⅞ inches   Signed EK
Gold mark crossed anchors
AKS plate 280

110 BELL-PUSH, composed of a solid cube of pale green bowenite decorated with dull green gold foliate mounts and red gold arrows set with rose diamonds. A pink-stained Mecca stone forms the push within a gold border chased with leaves, berries and roses.
2 inches square   Signed МП
AKS plate 146

111 Carved rock crystal HAND SEAL formed as a square-sectioned column with chamfered corners hung with red and dull green chased gold foliate swags and border and set with four carbuncles.
Height 1⅝ inches   No marks

112 Rock crystal rectangular BOX, the two hinged lids opening diagonally at the top, with yellow gold mounts set with four triangular-cut cabochon rubies.
Length 2½ inches   Signed МП
Gold mark crossed anchors

113 Elongated oval red gold BOX, engine-turned with green gold chased laurel borders in the Louis XVI manner, the hinged cover and base set with bevelled panels of carved rock crystal.
Length 2 3/16 inches   Signed МП

114 Pale smoky crystal-quartz CIGARETTE BOX; the engraved yellow gold mount which forms the hinged bezel is chased with leaves enamelled pale translucent emerald over veined engraving, allowing the gold on the tip of each leaf to be seen; this border is set at intervals with rose diamond ties.
Length 3 inches   Signed МП

CASE J

Objects from the collection at Sandringham lent by gracious permission
of Her Majesty The Queen.

J1 Rectangular hinged silver BOX, with chamfered corners, enamelled translucent pale green over a wavy *guilloché* ground, with red and green chased gold foliate and Vitruvian scroll borders, with flower-heads set with rose diamonds; a rose diamond thumb-piece.
Length 4¾ inches   Signed К. ФАБЕРЖЕ

J2 Silver SNUFF BOX, with chamfered corners enamelled translucent deep red over a wavy engraved ground, with chased red and green gold laurel mounts, the hinged cover surmounted by a gold Catherine the Great rouble within a frame of rose diamonds.
Length 2½ inches   Signed МП

J3 Rectangular silver POWDER BOX enamelled overall in opalescent oyster over an engraved field, chased with red and green gold laurel borders. Three hinged lids, each with a rose diamond thumb-piece, open to reveal inside six compartments and a looking glass. A small enamelled gold-mounted implement with a moonstone knop fits into one of the compartments.
Length 4 inches   Signed A★H

J4 Purpurine BOX, mounted in red gold, the hinged lid with a rounded opaque white-enamelled border crossed at intervals by translucent emerald-enamelled leaf ties. [63]

1⅞ inches square   Gold mark 72
Signed HW
AKS plate 188

J5 Heart-shaped rock crystal BOX, the cover, mounted in yellow gold, inset with a pale rose-coloured agate engraved with an Arabic inscription, bordered by a band of translucent emerald green enamel set with rose diamonds.
Length 1 9/16 inches
Gold mark crossed anchors
Signed МП

J6 Small rectangular COMFIT BOX, in engraved yellow gold enamelled translucent pale pink over wave-patterned engraving, bordered by opaque white-enamelled lines and decorated with chased green gold swags set with rose diamonds. The hinged cover inset with a moss-agate panel within a frame of half pearls, with a rose diamond thumb-piece. [63]
Length 1 7/16 inches   Gold mark 72
Signed HW
AKS colour plate XXX

J7 Smoky-quartz heart-shaped BOX, with yellow gold mount, bordered by rose diamonds, with a cabochon ruby thumb-piece.
Length 1¾ inches   Signed МП
AKS plate 188

J8 Rectangular purpurine BOX, mounted in engraved red gold with chased green gold laurel border within opaque enamelled white lines.
Length 2¾ inches   Gold mark 72
Signed HW
AKS plate 188

J9 Circular BOX, in engraved red gold enamelled translucent royal blue over an engraved ground, with green gold chased borders, the cover applied with a rose diamond basket of flowers set with three cabochon rubies and two emeralds. [63]
Diameter 1½ inches   Gold mark 72
Signed HW
AKS colour plate XXX

J10 Red-brown carved cornelian BOX, mounted in yellow gold in the form of a pumpkin, the removable segment with a border enamelled opaque white and set with rose diamonds.
Diameter 2⅛ inches [63]
Gold mark 72 and crossed anchors
Signed ФАБЕРЖЕ
Any workmaster's initials there may originally have been, are now worn away.
AKS plate 128

J11 Gold-mounted silver COMFIT BOX, enamelled translucent magenta over a *guilloché* background with red and green gold chased laurel

border, the hinged cover with a rose diamond at its centre.
1½ inches square   Signed МП

J12 LETTER-OPENER, of scimitar form, the curved blade of bowenite; the handle, mounted in yellow gold, is enamelled translucent strawberry over a wavy engraved field and is set with rose diamonds and three pearls.
Length 3⅞ inches   No marks

J13 COMBINED LETTER-OPENER AND PAPER-CLIP, mounted in red and green golds; the handle, decorated with a diamond pattern of translucent strawberry and opaque white enamels, is set with three rose diamonds and is fitted, at the back, with an engraved clip. The blade is carved in Siberian nephrite.
Length 4¹³⁄₁₆ inches   Signed МП

J14 LETTER-OPENER mounted in red and green golds, the tubular handle is enamelled translucent green with a carbuncle finial and fitted with a gold clip at the back. The blade is of carved rock crystal.
Length 3¾ inches   No marks

J15 Bowenite SCENT FLACON, in the Chinese style, carved as a mask, mounted in dull yellow gold and set with rose diamonds, with a brilliant diamond push-piece and surmounted by a cabochon ruby.
Height 2⁷⁄₁₆ inches   Signed К. ФАБЕРЖЕ

J16 Another SCENT FLACON similar to the previous exhibit, in nephrite mounted in yellow gold and set with rose diamonds and a cabochon ruby. A scent flacon very like this one, but with a pearl finial and signed by Wigström, is illustrated in AKS, plates 67 and 68.
Height 2⁷⁄₁₆ inches   No marks

J17 A third SCENT FLACON, carved in green aventurine-quartz mounted in yellow gold and set with rose diamonds and a cabochon ruby.
Height 2⁷⁄₁₆ inches   No marks

J18 PAPER-CLIP in engraved red and green golds; the triangular mount is enamelled translucent strawberry over a *guilloché* sunray and an opaque white enamel border. The stubby blade is carved in bowenite.
Length 2¹¹⁄₁₆ inches   Signed МП

J19 LETTER-OPENER, with a carved nephrite blade, surmounted by a white quartzite carving of an elephant with tiny cabochon ruby eyes, in an engraved yellow gold fringed mount set with rose diamonds and sapphires and with a sapphire polished to a point as a finial on its back. It stands upon a gold platform enamelled translucent strawberry and opaque white and has a ring of rose diamonds at its base. A reference to the Royal Danish Elephant and a complement to Marie Feodorovna who had been a Danish princess.
Length 5¾ inches   Signed МП
Gold mark crossed anchors
AKS colour plate XXX

J20 LETTER-OPENER, with a carved nephrite blade and gold-mounted handle enamelled in an alternating scallop pattern of translucent strawberry and opalescent oyster over engraved grounds. A border of chased red and green gold joins the handle to the blade.
Length 5³⁄₁₆ inches   No marks
AKS colour plate XXX

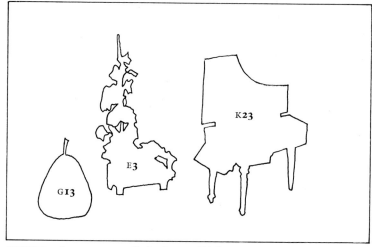

OVERLEAF ▲   OPPOSITE *Left* F8, F9   *Right* K2

60

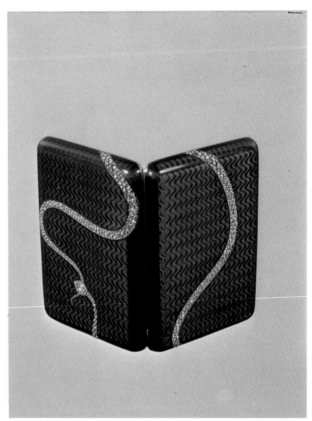

CASE K

Objects lent by gracious permission of Her Majesty The Queen and other articles of Royal provenance.

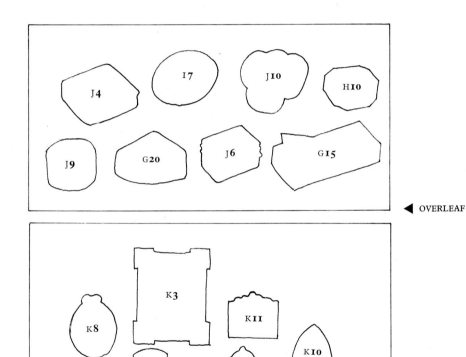

◀ OVERLEAF

◀ OPPOSITE

K1 Silver CIGARETTE CASE of oval section enamelled matt cyclamen, with two chased red and green gold foliate borders, a push-piece and mount set with rose diamonds.
Length 3⅜ inches Signed HW
HCB plate 120

K2 Red gold double-opening CIGARETTE CASE, enamelled royal-blue over a *guilloché moiré* ground, encircled by an inlaid snake composed of rose diamonds set as scales in pale green gold. An elliptical diamond forms the push-piece. This imaginatively designed case was given to Edward VII by Mrs George Keppel. After the King's death, Queen Alexandra generously returned it to the donor as a souvenir. In 1936, Mrs Keppel, in turn, gave it to Queen Mary 'to place with the Russian collection of Fabergé things at Sandringham'. A note in Queen Mary's hand, setting out this history, is enclosed inside the case. [61]
Height 3$\frac{11}{16}$ inches Signed К. ФАБЕРЖЕ
HCB plate 69

K3 Rectangular red gold MINIATURE FRAME, with sides cut away to form squares at the corners, enamelled translucent deep violet over a *guilloché* sunray ground; the oval aperture which contains a painted portrait of the Tsarina, Marie Feodorovna, as a young woman, rests upon a decorative shelf supporting a lavish ribboned sheaf of flowers in

four colours of gold which surrounds the miniature. [64]
Height 3¾ inches   Signed MΠ
Gold mark crossed anchors
HCB plate 88   AKS plate 85

K4 Miniature ÉSCRITOIRE in Louis XVI style, in yellow gold with pierced borders and chased red gold mounts and floral swags, enamelled translucent red-brown on a ground specially engraved to simulate the grain of the veneer. Decorated with two panels enamelled with classical motifs *en grisaille* and, at the corners, eight smaller panels with the Imperial cypher of Marie Feodorovna, all with a background of opaque enamelled turquoise to give the effect of Sèvres porcelain plaques. The hinged mother-of-pearl top is engraved with four double-headed eagles, and the small circular panel below with a rose. This must be one of Fabergé's most carefully observed pastiches.
Height 3½ inches   Signed MΠ
AKS colour plate LIV

K5 CHELSEA PENSIONER, with aventurine quartz face and hands, purpurine overcoat, black Siberian jasper hat and boots, gun-metal cuffs, translucent brown enamelled stick, enamelled medals, gold buttons and set with cabochon sapphire eyes.
Height 4⁵⁄₁₆ inches   No marks
AKS plate 263

K6 Siberian jade demi-lune MINIATURE-FRAME, designed as an open fan, in yellow, red and green chased gold mounts; the 'sticks' join at a rose diamond-set pinion and the oval frame, bordered by half-pearls, hangs from a series of foliate swags. The photograph is that of the Hon. Julia Stonor, later Marquise d'Hautpoul.

Towards the end of the 90's, the Prince of Wales, who tired easily in exclusively male company, was, according to Lady Geraldine Somerset, 'more or less in love' with Julie Stonor, the daughter of Mrs Francis Stonor, lady-in-waiting to the Princess of Wales.
Length 6⁵⁄₁₆ inches   Signed MΠ
AKS plate 167

K7 Engraved rock crystal STRUT MINIATURE-FRAME, the circular engraved gold bezel enamelled opalescent pink and crossed, at intervals, by rose diamond ties.
2⅝ inches square   Signed MΠ
Gold mark crossed anchors

K8 Oval red gold MINIATURE-FRAME, with chased green gold vertical stripes of laurel overlaying an engraved field enamelled translucent pale cerulean blue, surmounted by a red gold ribbon tied in a bow-knot. It contains a photograph of Princess Maud of Wales, later Princess Charles of Denmark and Queen of Norway. [64]
Height 2⁷⁄₁₆ inches   Signed MΠ
AKS plate 85

K9 Rectangular red gold MINIATURE-FRAME, with a triangular top, enamelled translucent deep red over engraving and hung with chased floral swags in golds of three colours and set with pearls. The photograph shows Elizabeth Feodorovna, Grand Duchess Sergei Alexandrovitch of Russia, possibly during the First World War, as a nursing sister. This tiny strut frame and the subsequent six examples by Viktor Aarne are all backed with mother-of-pearl instead of the more usual ivory. [64]
Height 1¹¹⁄₁₆ inches   Signed BA

K10 Engraved red gold MINIATURE-FRAME, shaped as a medieval arch, enamelled translucent green over an engraved background, it is embellished with a three-colour gold swag with garlands set with two rose diamonds. The photograph shows Alexandra, Princess of Wales, with her granddaughters, Lady Alexandra Duff (left) and Lady Maud Duff (right), the daughters of Princess Louise and the Duke of Fife. [64]
Height 1¹¹⁄₁₆ inches   Signed BA
AKS plate 85

K11 Two hinged red gold rectangular MINIATURE-FRAMES, on chased gold feet, surmounted by a scrolling gold ribbon forming a bow-knot with, as its central pivot, a pineapple finial. Each frame, enamelled translucent royal blue over sunray engraving, is decorated with three-colour gold chased swags and set with three half-pearls and has oval borders set with rose diamonds. The photographs are of Prince Charles of Denmark (later King Haakon VII of Norway) and his future wife Princess Maud of Wales. [64]
Height 1¹⁵⁄₁₆ inches   Signed BA
AKS plate 85

K12 A rectangular red gold MINIATURE-FRAME, composed of interesting rods enamelled opaque white between fine gold lines each set with a pearl at either end and entwined with elaborately chased garlands in three colours of gold. The framed mount is enamelled opalescent pale pink over sunray engraving, the oval aperture is bordered by half-pearls and contains a photograph of Princess Louise (later Princess Royal), Duchess of Fife. [64]
Height 1¹⁵⁄₁₆ inches   Signed BA
AKS plate 85

K13 Red gold rectangular MINIATURE-FRAME with a curved top, enamelled translucent pale lilac over an engraved field and set with half-pearls. The photograph is not very clear, but the subjects appear to be Alexandra, Princess of Wales (left) and Queen Olga of the Hellenes (right). [64]
Height 1 $\frac{11}{16}$ inches   Signed BA

K14 Shaped carved nephrite MINIATURE-FRAME, hung with three-colour gold garlands and swags. The rectangular aperture, bordered by rose diamonds, is surmounted by a scrolling bow-knot and the frame is set with four cabochon rubies and contains a photograph of Albert Edward, Prince of Wales, later King Edward VII. [64]
Height 1 $\frac{9}{16}$ inches   Signed BA
AKS plate 85

K15 Red gold MINIATURE-FRAME with concave sides and a domed top, enamelled translucent aquamarine over sunray engraving, surmounted by scrolling gold ribbon and hung with three-colour chased gold swags secured by four pearls. The oval aperture is edged with rose diamonds and contains a photograph of Maud, Princess Charles of Denmark, later Queen of Norway. [64]
Height 1 $\frac{11}{16}$ inches   Signed BA
AKS plate 85

K16 Red gold CIGARETTE CASE, with a ribbed sunburst design which radiates from a single brilliant diamond. It is fitted with a match compartment and tinder attachment and the thumb-piece is set with a cabochon saphire. This was a favourite case of the Tsar, Nicholas II.
Length 3 $\frac{5}{8}$ inches   Signed A★H
HCB plate 118   AKS plate 199

K17 Red gold CIGARETTE CASE, reeded in a sunray pattern, with some rays chased in green gold, with a match compartment and tinder attachment. The thumb-piece is set with a cabochon ruby.
Length 3 $\frac{3}{4}$ inches   Signed A★H
HCB plate 117

K18 Palisander wood CIGARETTE CASE, applied on either side with a red and green gold chased panel with a winged sphinx set against an enamelled background of opalescent oyster over engraving. Set with a moonstone push-piece. [42]
Length 4 inches   Signed МΠ

K19 Double opening CIGARETTE CASE, in carved rhodonite mounted in gold and set with rose diamonds. This attractive rose-coloured stone is sometimes known by its Russian name, *orletz*.
Length 3 $\frac{5}{16}$ inches   Signed HW
HCB plate 117

K20 Silver-gilt shaped MINIATURE-FRAME, enamelled a very pale translucent blue, the aperture bordered by opaque white enamel. Embellished with chased mounts in four colours of gold and set with five cabochon rubies, it contains a photograph of the Tsarevitch, Alexis Nicolaevitch of Russia.
Height 4 $\frac{5}{16}$ inches   Signed BA

K21 Rectangular red gold and leather WRITING-BLOCK COVER, with a chased green gold border and an elaborate oval chased foliate miniature frame with ribbons and tassels, set with two small rose diamonds, applied to the main area which is enamelled translucent pink over a *guilloché moiré* ground. The pencil,

in reeded red gold, is set with a blue Mecca stone knop.
Length 4 inches   Signed HW
AKS plate 188

K22 PRESENTATION BOX in gold, enamelled on cover and sides in translucent blue-grey over engraving and mounted with a chased green and red gold border. The hinged cover is applied with a miniature portrait of Nicholas II within a rose diamond frame surmounted by the Imperial Crown in brilliant and rose diamonds. The sunray panel of blue-grey enamel is bordered by a broad path enamelled opalescent oyster, set with ten brilliant diamonds at intervals and edged on either side by rose diamonds. The Tsar gave this box to General Trepov. [51]
Length 3 $\frac{3}{4}$ inches   Signed HW
Gold mark 72
HCB colour plate 7

K23 MINIATURE GRAND PIANO in Siberian jade, mounted in green and red gold, decorated with chased swags. When the top is opened, the keyboard, composed of opaque black and white enamelled keys, is revealed; it is surmounted by a panel bearing the name C. Fabergé inscribed in sepia enamel over a background of opalescent oyster. [62]
Length 2 $\frac{13}{16}$ inches   Signed МΠ
AKS plate 281

K24 Gold PRESENTATION BOX with all its rectangular sides enamelled opalescent oyster, with a hint of flame over *guilloché* grounds and bordered by a fine line of opaque white enamel, the main borders in granulated gold 'jewelled' with opalescent enamelled pellets and translucent emerald leaves in sprays centred on ruby enamelled lozenges.

The hinged cover, with an oval plaque bordered by Vitruvian scrolling enamelled opaque white over a translucent red ground, is set with an enamel-painting *en grisaille* heightened with sepia of the Peter the Great monument signed and dated by Zuiev, 1913. The box is mounted with a brilliant and rose diamond thumb-piece. [51]
Length 3⅝ inches   Signed HW
HCB colour plate 7

K1 to K24 lent by gracious permission of Her Majesty The Queen.

K25 Pair of red gold CUFF-LINKS, in the form of dumb-bells, each dumb-bell enamelled translucent royal blue over engraving within rose diamond borders and set at either end with rock crystals cut cabochon.
Length of each link ⅞ inch   Signed AT
His Royal Highness The Prince of Wales.

K25

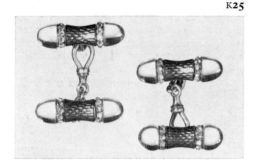

K26 RIDING CROP, with a carved Siberian jade handle with a collar enamelled translucent strawberry over an engraved wavy ground and mounted with chased green gold laurel borders.
Height of handle 1½ inches   Signed HW
Her Royal Highness The Princess Anne, Mrs Mark Phillips.

K26

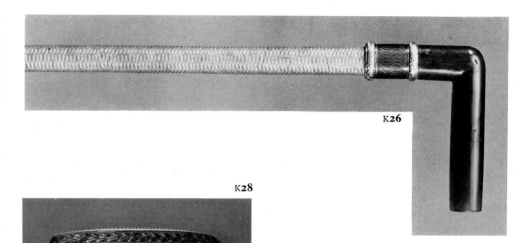

K28

K27 Pair of gold-mounted rock crystal TOILET BOTTLES, engraved with floral motifs and hung with chased bow-knots, garlands and swags in red, green and white golds. The globular chased gold stoppers enamelled opalescent rose and oyster, each with a cabochon sapphire finial. Compare with a similar pair of bottles in AKS plate 184
Height 5½ inches   Signed KΦ

K28 Gold CIGARETTE CASE decorated with opaque white enamelled lines with a brilliant diamond push-piece and borders of leaves enamelled translucent emerald with rose-diamond ties and at the centre, a basket of flowers in rose-diamonds over an opaque enamelled background.
Height 3 3/16 inches   Gold mark 72
Signed HW
HCB plate 107

K27 and K28, Her Royal Highness, The Princess Margaret, Countess of Snowdon.

68

K27

K29

K29 CIGARETTE CASE with match compartment and tinder attachment in yellow gold, composed largely of the original embossed and chased panels of a *Régence* card case.
Length 3⅞ inches   Signed МП
Gold marks 72 and crossed anchors
HCB plate 102   AKS plate 53
His Royal Highness, The Duke of Kent.

K30 Circular red gold STRUT CLOCK with chased green gold acanthus borders, enamelled translucent peach over a wavy *guilloché* ground, the circumference is divided into twelve panels enamelled opalescent white on sunray backgrounds, embellished with simulated moss-agate motifs in painted sepia enamel. The dial is framed by half-pearls and the hands are of pierced gold.
Her Highness Princess Anne of Denmark.
Diameter 5 inches   Signed МП
Her Highness Princess Anne of Denmark.

K31 Red and green gold CIGARETTE CASE fluted with a deeply incised sunray pattern. At the centre of the cover, a circular plaque bordered by rose diamonds and enamelled translucent royal blue over an engraved sun-in-splendour is applied with the crowned monogram of The Grand Duke Nicolai Nicolaievitch in rose diamonds. The thumbpiece is set with a cabochon sapphire. 'Nicolasha' as he was known, was Commander in Chief of the Army in the 1914 war until Nicholas II, so ill-advisedly, himself took over late in 1915.
Length 3½ inches   Signed A★H

K31

K32

K32

K32 Small red gold HAND SEAL in the form of a bowenite egg supported upon a flared stem enamelled translucent peach over an engraved ground terminating in a base encircled by chased green gold laurel. Engraved for sealing with the crowned monogram AH of the Tsarevitch Alexis Nicolaievitch, whose personal seal this was.
Height 1 7/16 inches   Signed ФА

CASE L

The objects in this case form part of the Forbes Magazine collection, New York.

L1 Standing double-sided MINIATURE-FRAME in the form of a fire-screen with chased floral swags and trophies in five colours of gold. The framework, enamelled opaque white *champlevé*, is set with two oriental pearl finials; the rectangular frame itself is enamelled opalescent oyster on one side against a scalloped ground, with an oval photograph of Nicholas II within a half-pearl border. The reverse, enamelled opalescent pale rose, holds a photograph of the Tsarina, similarly framed.
Height 7 inches   Signed HW
Gold mark 72
AKS colour plate XXVII

L2 CHANTICLEER EGG, probably presented to the Dowager Empress Marie Feodorovna by Nicholas II. Probable date, 1903. In the French neo-classical manner, this graceful Egg is enamelled translucent Cambridge blue over a *guilloché* surface of gold. Heavy chased green gold laurel swags hang from a circular pierced gold grille at the top, and a line of pearls within borders of chased green gold leaves and berries forms a belt around the centre of the Egg; this belt is interrupted by the opalescent white enamelled dial of the clock set in gold within a ring of pearls. The hands are of gold and the numerals are painted in blue enamel. The Egg is mounted on a four-sided pedestal decorated with applied

Fabergé's workshop showing the Chanticleer Egg (L2) on the bench.

red and green gold devices of the Arts and Sciences. The four main concave panels are enamelled translucent blue while the remaining one bordering them and the fluted shaft supporting the Egg, are opalescent white.

The diamond-set cockerel in gold and vari-coloured enamels which rises from the interior of the Egg, flapping its wings and crowing, does not do so at the pressure of a button, but automatically at each hour. When it has announced the time, it disappears beneath the grille which closes down over the top of the Egg. [81]
Height 11 inches   Signed MΠ

L3 Imperial presentation FRAME with a photograph of Nicholas II in gold set with rock crystal panels engraved with entwined trails of laurel, the borders chased in high relief with enamelled translucent emerald crossed at intervals by opaque white-enamelled ties. The four square panels and six roundels between them, enamelled opalescent pink over sunray engraving, are applied with four-colour gold chased motifs set with rose diamonds; those at the corners, the Imperial Crown; at the top, the cypher of Marie Feodorovna; below, the Romanov double-headed eagle; the sides each with two trophies. The silver-gilt scroll strut is applied with the Imperial Crown.
Height 14⅝ inches   Signed MΠ

L4 ORANGE-TREE EGG, presented to the Dowager Empress Marie Feodorovna by Nicholas II. Date 1911. In the form of an orange tree growing in a tub, this Easter Egg is a remarkable example of the jeweller's art. Set upon a solid block of nephrite and surrounded by four gold-mounted nephrite pillars connected by swinging chains of translucent emerald-enamelled gold leaves half covering pearls. A white quartz tub, set with cabochon rubies and pearls, trellised in gold and decorated with chased gold swags, is filled with hammered gold soil. As if growing from this soil, a naturalistically modelled gold tree trunk sup-

71

ports the egg-shaped foliage composed of single carved nephrite leaves, each engraved to show the veining. White opaque enamel flowers with brilliant diamond centres and various green stones including topaz, amethysts, pale rubies and champagne diamonds representing fruit, are set at random amongst the leaves. Within this nephrite foliage, four main limbs, branch from the trunk, and a complex network of smaller branches grows from these, each finally passing through tiny drilled collets concealed behind each leaf. When a small button is pressed, the top leaves spring up and a feathered gold bird rises from the interior of the tree, sings and then automatically disappears. The key to the mechanism is hidden among the leaves and may be located only by the gem set in the top disguised as another fruit. [81]
Height 10½ inches   No marks

L5   TABLE CLOCK in nephrite, with a silver-gilt cartouche enamelled translucent pale pink on an engraved sunray field, with red and green chased gold foliate borders with ribbons and bow-knots set with rose diamonds; a circular pendant cartouche has at its centre Roman numerals indicating that this was a twenty-fifth anniversary gift. The dial, enamelled opalescent oyster over an engraved sunburst, is bordered by half-pearls and is fitted with pierced red gold hands.
Height 6½ inches   Signed HW
AKS plate 142

L6   Gold miniature TANKARD with gadrooned borders, the body applied with eight coins of five roubles and four of two roubles, the hinged cover with a five rouble piece. The

scroll handle and thumb-piece are each set with a cabochon sapphire. The coins date from 1758 to 1783.
Height 3¼ inches   Gold mark crossed anchors
Signed EK

L7   FIFTEENTH ANNIVERSARY EGG, presented to Alexandra Feodorovna by Nicholas II, dated 1911. The following is based on a translation of the description given with a photograph of this egg, printed in *Stolitza y Usadba* (Town and Country), 'The Journal of Elegant Living', a magazine published in what was then Petrograd. This particular issue, dated 1st April, 1916, gave special prominence to a series of photographs of nine of the Tsarina's Easter Eggs:

Red gold Egg commemorating the fifteenth anniversary of Nicholas II's Coronation; it is enamelled opalescent oyster with heavy carved husk borders enamelled translucent emerald green with diamond ties at the intersections. The surface is covered with a series of miniature paintings on ivory by Zuiev depicting notable events of the reign; these are set under carved rock crystal panels and represent:

1 The ceremonial procession to the Uspensky Cathedral.
2 The actual moment of the Holy Coronation.
3 The Alexander III bridge in Paris at the opening of which His Imperial Majesty was present.
4 The House in the Hague, where the first Peace Conference took place, Huis ten Bosch.

L7

5 The ceremonial reception for the members of the first State Duma in the Winter Palace.
6 The Emperor Alexander III Museum.
7 The unveiling of the Peter the Great monument in Riga.
8 The unveiling in Poltava of the monument commemorating the 200th year of the founding of Poltava.
9 The removal of the remains of the sainted Serafim Sarovski.

The paintings are framed by narrow opaque

L7

L7

Egg is enamelled translucent strawberry on a *guilloché* field. It is richly embellished with chased green gold *rocaille* decoration in the Louis XV manner and the red gold rim which bisects the Egg is set with rose diamonds, as are the two surmounting fasteners. When these are divided the Easter Egg opens to reveal the surprise, a basket of spring flowers on a small gold circular plinth. The flowers are carved in milky chalcedony with olivine centres set in green gold, and the gold leaves are enamelled translucent green over an engraved ground. The basket, which is chased in platinum, is elaborately pierced and set with a profusion of rose diamonds, as is the handle.

This flower-basket motif was used again much later by Fabergé in his Winter Egg of 1913. As in the case of all the early Imperial Easter Eggs, this example is smaller than those which were made in 1896 and after.

Height of Egg 3 inches
Height of basket $1\frac{5}{16}$ inches
Gold mark crossed anchors
Signed МП

white enamelled borders with oval portrait miniatures of the Imperial Family are set in opalescent oyster enamelled mounts over *guilloché* fields and rimmed by rose diamonds.

Fabergé's signature appears twice in pale blue enamel in three parts (ФА, БЕР, ЖЕ) on a ribbon on the plaques showing the dates 1894 (the date of the wedding) and 1911, below pink bouquets. The chased acanthus mounts encircling the rose diamond cluster at the culot of the Egg, and the portrait and rose diamond cluster at the top, under which is the Imperial Cypher АФ beneath the crown, are in dull green gold.

Height $5\frac{1}{8}$ inches   No gold marks
AKS plates 365 and 366

L8 SPRING FLOWER EGG, presented to Marie Feodorovna by Alexander III, made between 1885 and 1890. Supported on a circular carved and fluted bowenite base, mounted with red and green gold scrolls and chased acanthus leaves and set with rose diamonds, the gold

L9 Carved nephrite gold-mounted PRESEN-TATION BOX, with a chased red and green gold foliate border. The hinged cover enriched with a rose diamond trellis set in silver with, at its centre, a foliate wreath surrounding a miniature painting of Nicholas II wearing the Order of St George, by Zuiev, within a frame of rose diamonds and surmounted by the Imperial Crown in diamonds.

Length $3\frac{3}{4}$ inches   Signed HW
HCB plate 127   AKS plate 130

L10 A BASKET, with looped handle in plaited gold wire, filled with rough green gold moss

from which grows groups of lily-of-the-valley in gold and oriental pearls, the leaves carved in nephrite. Formerly in the collection of Princess Marina, Duchess of Kent. [82]
Height 3¼ inches   Signed MΠ
Gold mark crossed anchors
AKS colour plate LXV

L11   Siberian nephrite one-piece carving of a WATERING-CAN, with a gold handle and rose enamelled translucent strawberry on an engraved ground and set with rose diamond borders. Originally part of the collection of Elizabeth Balletta of the Imperial Michael Theatre.
Length 4⅛ inches   No marks
AKS colour plate XXIX

L12   CROSS OF ST GEORGE EGG, presented to the Dowager Empress Marie Feodorovna by Nicholas II, dated 1916. This Egg was made to commemorate the recent presentation of the Order of St George to the Tsarevitch and the Cross of that Order to his father. In opalescent white enamel, the surface of this silver Egg is trellised with a simple laurel pattern forming panels within which military crosses of St George are painted. The Egg is encircled by the black and orange-striped ribbon of the Order of St George, which was awarded in recognition of outstanding courage; from two of the bows of this ribbon, which is carried out in enamel, hang silver medallions which may be raised upwards by pressing small buttons set beneath them, to reveal painted miniatures set in the main shell of the Egg. One medallion, showing the Tsar's head, covers the portrait of the Tsarevitch and the other, showing the Cross of St George, the portrait of the Tsar. The crowned initials of the Dowager

L12

Empress appear raised within a round carved border at the top of the Egg, while the year is similarly applied to the base.
Height 3 5/16 inches
ФАБЕРЖЕ engraved on the edge of the medallion with the Tsar's head.

L13   Figure of a DRUNKEN MUJIK (peasant) dancing, the tunic in purpurine, trousers yellow jasper, cap and boots in black jasper, hands and face in pinky agate and hair and beard in grey jasper. Eyes set with cabochon

sapphires and a twisted gold wire round his waist.
Height 5¼ inches
Illus. in colour, *The Connoisseur*, June 1962.

L14   Miniature SEDAN CHAIR in red gold, with panels enamelled translucent rose on sunray backgrounds with sepia-painted symbols of the arts. Enamelled with opaque white and translucent emerald green rosettes and granulated borders, chased yellow gold mounts, engraved rock crystal bevelled windows and lined with mother-of-pearl. The detachable carrying poles in reeded gold are mounted at either end with mother-of-pearl handles and a chased gold handle, when turned, opens the door.
Height 3⅝ inches   Gold mark 72   Signed MΠ
AKS colour plate L

L15   EGG IN THE RENAISSANCE STYLE, presented to Marie Feodorovna by Alexander III. Dated 1894. Clearly based on Le Roy's masterpiece in the *Grune Gewölbe* at Dresden, this Easter Egg in the Renaissance style is carved from a large block of milky grey agate to form a jewel casket. A scalloped border in rose diamonds at the top of the cover encloses a strawberry-coloured translucent enamel medallion with the year in diamonds. The Egg, which is mounted horizontally on an enamelled gold base, is richly decorated with a trellis pattern and numerous other gold motifs enamelled strawberry, emerald green, cerulean blue, opaque white and is set with an abundance of rose diamonds and cabochon rubies. The clasp is set with rose diamonds. Chased gold lions' heads holding rings in their mouths are mounted at either end of this. The last Easter Egg given to Marie Feodorovna by her husband. The surprise has been lost.

In comparing Fabergé's work with Le Roy's, note how carefully the modern goldsmith has carried out an almost identical composition in a far lighter vein, by means of a subtle appreciation of the basic egg shape and a careful adjustment of the scales as instanced by the gentle curve added to the trellis pattern, and the more substantial base in relation to the casket as a whole. [81]

Length 5¼ inches   Signed МП
Gold mark crossed anchors
HCB plate 63   AKS colour plate LXXII and plate 324

L16 Oval Louis XVI SNUFF-BOX in engraved red gold, enamelled translucent scarlet and with a very similar décor to the Fabergé box (L17), which is based upon this example. By Joseph Etienne Blerzy, Paris, 1777
Length 3¼ inches
AKS plate 52

Casket by Le Roy of Amsterdam, early 18th century, from which L15 is derived. Green Vaults, Dresden.

L17 Oval SNUFF-BOX, in engraved red gold enamelled translucent green, with granulated gold borders decorated with opalescent pellets, leaves and berries in translucent green and red enamel. The hinged cover is applied with an eighteenth century plaque enamelled *en grisaille* with an allegorical scene framed with rose diamonds. This box is designed as a pastiche based on the French example (L16), was made by Fabergé in answer to a challenge by Alexander III, who declared that, in his opinion, the Paris goldsmiths of the eighteenth century could not be equalled. When he saw the new box, the Tsar was so impressed that he ordered both the original and the 'copy' to be exhibited side by side in the Hermitage.
Length 3¼ inches   Signed МП
Gold marks 72 and crossed anchors
AKS colour plate IX

CASE M

Objects from the India Early Minshall collection of the Cleveland Museum of Art, the Matilda Geddings Gray Foundation collection, New Orleans, and from individual private collections.

M1 TRIANGULAR FRAME composed of three reeded gold intersecting poles each with a cabochon ruby set at either end. Elaborately chased floral garlands with ribbons in four colours of gold form a pendant within which a rose diamond bordered frame hangs, containing a miniature painting of the Tsarina Alexandra Feodorovna. [102]
Height 5 $\frac{3}{16}$ inches   Signed К. ФАБЕРЖЕ
AKS colour plate XIX

M2 RED CROSS EGG WITH RESURRECTION TRIPTYCH, presented to Alexandra Feodorovna by Nicholas II. Dated 1915. In white opalescent enamel on an engraved silver-gilt ground, this gold-mounted Egg is emblazoned with a bold red translucent enamel cross on either side. The centre of each cross is set with circular painted miniature portraits of respectively the Grand Duchess Olga and Tatiana in Red Cross uniform. The front cross with the portrait of Tatiana serves as a clasp securing the double-opening doors, which reveal within a triptych painting by Prachov, with the Resurrection of Christ in the centre, and the Saints Olga and Tatiana painted on the side panels. The two remaining panels of the doors are inscribed, one with the crowned monogram of the Tsarina, and the other with the year 1915. The indifferent painting of the two unsigned exterior miniatures does not prepare one for

M2

76

the rather impressive triptych concealed within the Egg, thus, in this case, the 'surprise' is a double one. In order to save the Tsar money, the cost of this war-time 'austerity' egg was kept down to about £200.

Height 3⅜ inches Gold mark 72 Signed HW
AKS plates 378–381

M3 Pair of red and green gold rectangular MINIATURE FRAMES supported upon bowenite obelisks. The frames chased with foliate borders and swags in green gold and surmounted by pierced red gold scrolls, rosettes and shells, the stands each with entwined trails of laurel in chased green gold rising from a red gold ribbon bow-knot set with a small cabochon ruby.

The miniatures, which are both signed by Zehngraf, portray the Tsar Nicholas II and a baby, almost certainly the Grand Duchess Olga, his eldest child, born in 1895 and heir presumptive to the throne. This, taken together with the evidence of the crossed anchors gold mark, enables us to substantiate the date of the manufacture of these objects as 1896.

Height 6 inches Gold mark crossed anchors
Signed МП
AKS colour plate XVIII

M4 Standing TABLE CLOCK carved from a rectangular block of Siberian nephrite, the numerals represented in painted enamel by pink roses separated by translucent green-enamelled leaves, the hands set with rose diamonds. The clock is applied with four rose diamond mounts which appear to represent the Roman numeral III, the significance of which, if any, is not now known.

Height 3 1/16 inches Gold mark 72
Signed HW
AKS colour plate XXVIII

M4

M5 Miniature TEAPOT carved in light green jade and decorated with chased *repoussé* gold rococo scroll mounts. The cover with a finial designed as a *flambeau*.

Overall length 4¼ inches Signed МП
Gold mark crossed anchors

M6 Miniature chased dull gold SALT CHAIR in Louis XVI *cabriolet* style, designed as a commode. The hinged seat is carved from Siberian jade and is set with a panel simulating silk in opalescent oyster enamel with painted flowers,

scrolls and leaves in pale sepia over a *guilloché* ground. The back of the commode is set on both sides with oval panels similarly enamelled with trophies and entwined foliate borders, the front panel rimmed with half-pearls.

Height 3¼ inches Gold mark 72
Signed HW
HCB plate 38 AKS colour plate LII

M7 Miniature chased gold SALT CHAIR designed *à la reine*, the flowered upholstery painted in enamels to simulate brocade, set with two cabochon rubies and rose diamonds. The seat forms the lid of a receptacle, the hinge of which is cleverly concealed.

Height 4⅛ inches Signed К. ФАБЕРЖЕ
AKS colour plate LI

M1 to M7 are from the India Early Minshall collection of The Cleveland Museum of Art, U.S.A.

M8 EGG WITH DANISH PALACES AND RESIDENCES, presented to the Dowager Empress Marie Feodorovna by Nicholas II, probably 1895. A star sapphire within a cluster of rose diamonds and chased gold laurel leaves surmounts this *trois-couleur* gold Egg which is enamelled a translucent pink on a *guilloché* pattern of repeated crosses. The Egg is divided into twelve panels by broad bands consisting each of a line of rose diamonds within continuous laurel leaf borders chased in gold; an emerald is set at each intersection of the lines of rose diamonds.

A folding screen of miniature paintings framed in vari-coloured gold is recessed within the Egg. Painted on mother-of-pearl by Krijitski and dated 1891, eight of the ten panels depict palaces and residences in Denmark where the Dowager Empress, as Princess

M**8**

Dagmar, spent her childhood; the paintings at either end of the screen show the Imperial yachts *Standart* and *Poliarnaya Svesda*. The natural mother-of-pearl is vividly revealed when the miniatures are held up to the light. The date 1895 is written in ink on the outside of the velvet case containing this Egg.
Height 4 inches   Signed MΠ
Gold mark crossed anchors

M9 BASKET OF LILIES OF THE VALLEY in woven yellow gold. Nine sprays of lilies with engraved gold stalks, carved nephrite leaves and pearl and rose diamond flowers, grow in a bed of spun green gold and platinum simulating moss and executed in clipped wire, polished and unpolished in patches. The following is a translation of the Russian inscription engraved underneath the basket:

> To Her Imperial Majesty, Tsarina Alexandra Feodorovna from the Iron-works management and dealers in the Siberian iron section of the Nijegorodski Fair in the year 1896.

Height 7½ inches   Signed HW
Gold mark crossed anchors

M10 NAPOLEONIC EGG, presented to the Dowager Empress Marie Feodorovna by Nicholas II, dated 1912. In the Empire style, this green and yellow gold Egg commemorates the hundredth anniversary of the War of the Motherland waged against Napoleon. Military emblems and double-headed eagles chased in gold decorate the translucent emerald green with which the *guilloché* surface of the Egg is enamelled, and these are framed by broad bands of chased gold leaves and rosettes applied to translucent strawberry enamel. In addition to the profusion of rose diamonds

with which this magnificent Egg is set, portrait diamonds at either end cover the crowned monogram of the Dowager Empress and the date 1912.

Within the Egg is a folding screen of six signed miniatures by Vassily Zuiev, each showing members of the regiments of which Her Imperial Majesty was honorary Colonel; the back of each panel bears an inscription identifying these, and is set with her monogram and crown in rose diamonds on a green enamel plaque in the centre of a translucent white enamel sunburst pattern. Plate p. 86.
Height 4⅝ inches   Signed HW
AKS plates 370–372

M11 CHESTNUT LEAF realistically carved in Siberian nephrite with three berries in dull yellow gold clustered at the centre, one of which is partially open, revealing a cabochon almandine garnet.
Length 5 9/16 inches   No marks
HCB plate 26

M12 CAUCASUS EGG, presented to Marie Feodorovna by Alexander III, dated 1893. Mounted with *quatre-couleur* gold floral swags held by rose diamond bows, this splendid engraved gold Egg in Louis Seize style is enamelled a translucent crimson over an engraved field, with four pearl-bordered oval doors each bearing a diamond-set numeral of the year 1893 within a diamond wreath. The doors open to reveal painted views of Abastouman, a mountain retreat high in the Caucasus, signed by Krijitski. It was here that the Grand Duke George Alexandrovitch, the younger brother of Nicholas II, was obliged to spend the greater part of his life owing to his ill health. When the Egg is held to the light, through portrait diamonds at the top and base,

a miniature of the Grand Duke in naval uniform is seen. [82]
Height 3⅝ inches   Signed MΠ
Gold marks 72 and crossed anchors
AKS colour plate LXXI

M8 to M12 are from the Matilda Geddings Gray Foundation collection, New Orleans.

M13 PANSY EGG, presented to the Dowager Empress Marie Feodorovna by Nicholas II, dated 1899. Supported on a spiral twist of silver-gilt leaves and twigs set with rose diamonds, this carved nephrite Egg, designed in the *art nouveau* style, is decorated with opaque violet enamelled pansies, symbols of remembrance and affection. Inside is a gold easel surmounted by a diamond-set Star of Bethlehem within a wreath over the date; the easel is fluted and embellished with chased gold floral and torch motifs and is set with gems and pearls. On it rests a heart-shaped plaque enamelled opalescent white on a sunray *guilloché* background and bordered by rose diamonds set in silver and surmounted by the Romanov crown also in diamonds. Eleven tiny translucent strawberry enamelled gold covers, each bearing its own monogram, are connected by a large diamond 'M' to form a decoration for the front of this plaque. When a button is pressed, the enamelled covers open simultaneously to reveal eleven miniatures of the immediate Imperial Family. Reading vertically, those in the first row are: Grand Duke George, younger brother of the Tsar, Grand Duke Alexander, husband of the Grand Duchess Xenia, the Tsar's sister. In the second row are Tsar Nicholas II and Grand Duchess

OPPOSITE *Left* L4   *Above middle* O14   *Below middle* L15   *Right* L2

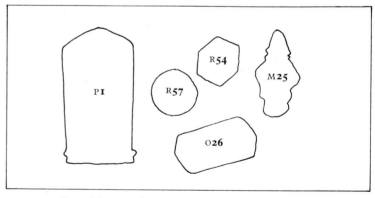

OVERLEAF *Above left* M12   *Above right* ▲
Below left P12   *Below right* L10

Irina, subsequently Princess Youssoupov, daughter of Grand Duke Alexander and Grand Duchess Xenia; in the third row, Grand Duchess Olga, the first child of the Tsar and Tsarina, Grand Duchess Tatiana, their second child, and Grand Duke Michael, youngest brother of the Tsar. The fourth row shows the Tsarina and Grand Duke Andrew, brother of Grand Duchess Irina, and the fifth, Grand Duchess Olga and Xenia, sisters of the Tsar.
Height of egg 5¾ inches   Signed MΠ
HCB plate 62   AKS plate 333

MI4 CUCKOO EGG, presented to Alexandra Feodorovna by Nicholas II, dated 1900. Easter egg clock in dull yellow, green and red golds, enamelled opalescent white and trans-lucent violet on a zig-zag *guilloché* field, set with pearls and rose diamonds. The dial, which is encircled by pearls set in red polished gold, is enamelled with translucent emerald green trefoils, and the rose diamond numerals are set on pale greenish white opalescent enamel within opaque white enamel rings. A yellow gold leaf pattern surrounds the central pivot on which the red gold hands revolve. The egg is supported on an elaborate base set with three large rose diamonds by a central shaft and three struts enamelled opalescent white. When a button at the back of the clock is pressed, the circular pierced gold grille which surmounts it opens and a cuckoo, plumed with natural feathers, set with cabo-chon ruby eyes and standing on gold legs, rises crowing on a gold platform. The beak and wings move authentically until, the crowing finished, it descends once again into the Egg, and the grille closes down. Surmounting this grille the date 1900 is inscribed beneath a portrait diamond.
Height 8⅜ inches   Signed MΠ
AKS colour plate LXXV
Mr and Mrs Bernard C. Solomon, Los Angeles.

MI5 Purpurine carving of a seated CAT, the eyes in yellow and black foiled rock crystal. This must be the largest piece of this material used for an animal sculpture.
Height 5 inches
AKS colour plate XXXVIII

MI6 Oval purpurine BOWL with dull yellow reeded gold handle and bezel with burnished red gold ribbon and bow-knots and set with two green garnets.
Length 3½ inches   Signed EK
HCB plate 101
Mr and Mrs Peter Thornton, U.S.A.

MI7 Carved striated agate CUP, mounted with a handle composed of two snakes in dull gold, their heads set respectively with a cabochon ruby and a cabochon sapphire.
Length 2¹⁵⁄₁₆ inches   Signed MΠ
Gold mark crossed anchors

MI8 Carved tawny aventurine-quartz ECUELLE with red and green gold chased and engraved mounts decorated in Renaissance style with opaque white enamel and set with emeralds and cabochon rubies.
Overall length 8¾ inches   Signed HW

OPPOSITE ▼   OVERLEAF O26

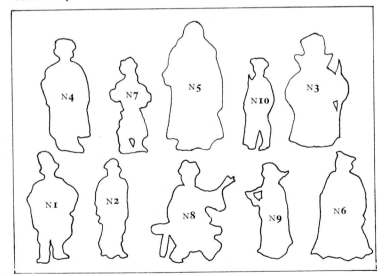

85

MI4

MI8

MI5

MI9

M20

M20 GATCHINA PALACE EGG, probably presented to the Dowager Empress Marie Feodorovna by Nicholas II, circa 1902. Enamelled opalescent white on a gold *guilloché* carcass, this superb egg is divided into twelve panels by lines of pearls. Portrait diamonds are set at either extremity, but unfortunately both the monogram and the year which, presumably, they once covered, have disappeared. Classical motifs painted in enamel in each of the segments refer to the various fields of endeavour actively and consistently encouraged by Marie Feodorovna. When the egg is opened, a wonderfully detailed model of the Gatchina Palace, near St Petersburg, is revealed; it is executed in four colours of gold,

M20

MI9 ROSE TRELLIS EGG, presented to either his wife or mother by Nicholas II, dated 1907. Gold easter egg in pale green translucent enamel, latticed with rose diamonds and decorated with opaque light and dark pink enamel roses and translucent emerald green leaves. A portrait diamond is set at either end of this very charming egg, the one at the base covering the date; unfortunately the monogram has disappeared from beneath the other. An oval jewelled locket was originally concealed in the egg, but now, unfortunately, only its impression on the satin lining remains.
Height 3 $\frac{1}{16}$ inches
Signed HW
HCB plate 42   AKS plates 351, 352

and under close scrutiny, shows trees, bridges, cannon, turrets and so on. This piece must be accounted one of Fabergé's most delightful compositions. Under the model of the palace, Marie Feodorovna's favourite residence, a velvet-lined space originally concealed a jewel now lost.
Height 5 inches
Signed MΠ
AKS plates 339, 340

MI9 and M20 Walters Art Gallery, Baltimore.

M21 Silver PEN-HOLDER enamelled translucent orange-rust over a wavy *guilloché* ground with red gold mount chased with green gold foliage.
Length 7 1/16 inches   Signed AR
This unidentified Fabergé workmaster, possibly active in Odessa or Kiev, is only known by his initials. See AKS, page 128.
Dr Edwin I. Radlauer, New York.

M22 Oviform purpurine PAPER-CLIP, with an engraved gold mount enamelled opaque white and translucent emerald and set with a moonstone.
Height 1 9/16 inches   Signed MΠ

M23 BONBONNIÈRE carved in smoky quartz in the form of a slice of crystallized fruit, the gold bezel decorated with translucent strawberry enamel over engraving and a band of rose diamonds.
Length 2 9/16 inches   Signed MΠ
AKS plate 143

M23

M24

M24 Engraved, gold-mounted, silver-gilt WHISTLE enamelled translucent pale blue over a *guilloché* field.
Length 1 1/2 inches   Unsigned

M25 A red gold-mounted SCENT BOTTLE, carved in parti-coloured cornelian of red-brown and grey in the form of a bearded gnome with his hands in the pockets of his overcoat. The eyes are two cabochon sapphires set in gold and the stocking cap, which acts as the hinged lid, is bordered by rose diamonds; when opened, the reeded gold stopper is revealed. The sculptor of this splendid one-piece carving has exploited the natural variations of the stone so that the face, hair and beard are all found where the material is of a grey-blue or grey-brown tone. The base is engraved as a hand-seal with the crowned monogram of the Tsarina, Alexandra Feodorovna. [82]
Height 3 inches   Signed KQ

M24 and M25 Mr and Mrs R. Kirk Landon, Florida.

M26 Carved bowenite SWIZZLE-STICK mounted in chased red and green gold and engraved on an applied gold plate with the monogram of Victoria Melita, Grand Duchess Cyril, beneath the Imperial crown and set with a cabochon amethyst knop. Shown in the original leather fitted case.
Length 5 1/2 inches   Signed HW
Mr and Mrs Oscar Getz, Chicago.

M27 BLUE ENAMEL RIBBED EGG, presented to Marie Feodorovna by Alexander III, made between 1885 and 1890. In three colours of gold and enamelled translucent royal blue, the egg is surmounted by an Imperial Crown set with sapphires and diamonds. Not an entirely successful design, despite some fine carving, this piece appears top-heavy partly owing to the excessive length of the finial, and partly to the inadequate base, which must originally have been much more substantial. The onyx steps supporting the egg are an addition to, or completion of, this light spiral gold stem. The surprise has been lost.
Height 4 1/4 inches   Signed MΠ
Gold mark crossed anchors
The Stavros S. Niarchos collection, Paris.

CASE N

N1 UKRAINIAN PEASANT (*hohol*) in aventurine-quartz, lapis-lazuli, white quartz, coffee jasper cloak, hair and moustache; cabochon sapphire eyes, obsidian hat and boots and purpurine belt, collar and front of quartzite shirt decorated with painted enamel, and holding a gold pipe. Engraved ФАБЕРЖЕ under left boot. [84]
Height 5⅜ inches
HCB colour plate 97   AKS colour plate XLV

N2 SOLDIER of the Preobrazhensky Regiment of His Imperial Majesty the Tsar in nephrite uniform and obsidian boots, hat in obsidian and nephrite, face and hands in aventurine-quartz, eyes in cabochon sapphires, rifle in gold and mountings in gold, silver and red translucent enamel. Engraved ФАБЕРЖЕ under right boot. [84]
Height 5 inches
Illustrated *The Connoisseur*, April 1936.

N3 NOBLEMAN (*boyarin*), coat in purpurine, the borders and collar in brown Caucasian sard, mountings chased in gold, hat in brown Caucasian sard and nephrite, shoes in nephrite, face in a prepared composition, hands in white quartzite, beard and hair in Siberian jasper, eyes in sapphires, staff in oxidised silver with gold knop and ferrule. Engraved ФАБЕРЖЕ under right shoe. [84]
Height 6 inches
HCB colour plate 98

N4 POLICEMAN (*gorodovoi*) in Caucasian uniform of obsidian quartzite, gloves and face in a prepared composition with cabochon sapphire eyes, mountings in gold, silver and enamel. The number 251 is applied in gold on the cap. Engraved ФАБЕРЖЕ under right boot. [84]
Height 6 inches
AKS colour plate XLV

N5 PEASANT (*mujik*) with face in a prepared composition, hair and beard in Norwegian sunstone, eyes in sapphires, overcoat in alabaster bordered by brown Caucasian sard, undershirt in quartzite, hat and boots in obsidian, belt in purpurine. The staff is in silver-gilt stamped HW88. Engraved ФАБЕРЖЕ under right boot. [84]
Height 6¾ inches
HCB colour plate 98
Wartski, London.

N6 COACHMAN of the nobility (*barski-kutcher*) in nephrite; belt and hat in purpurine, gloves in white quartz, face in aventurine quartz, mountings in gold. Engraved ФАБЕРЖЕ on base. [84]
Height 5 inches
Illustrated *The Connoisseur*, April 1936.

N7 CARPENTER (*plotnik*) with aventurine quartz face and arms, purpurine shirt, lapis-lazuli breeches, white quartz apron, brown jasper hair and beard, obsidian boots, cabochon sapphire eyes; he tests a gold and silver axe, the axe-head stamped HW and with silver mark 91. Engraved ФАБЕРЖЕ under right foot. [48]
Height 5 inches
HCB colour plate 97   AKS colour plate XLVII

N8 PEASANT (*mujik*), playing a silver-gilt balalaika, stamped HW and ФАБЕРЖЕ with the silver mark 88. Face and hands aventurine quartz, cabochon sapphire eyes, hair and moustache in stained cornelian, grey Kalgan jasper blouse, lapis-lazuli breeches, socks in quartzite, boots in Norwegian sunstone, bench in banded brown chalcedony. [84]
Height 4⅝ inches
HCB plate 100   AKS colour plate XLVII

N9 LABOURER (*zemlekop*) in purpurine, lapis-lazuli, with obsidian hat and boots, sard beard and hair, aventurine quartz face and hands, Norwegian sunstone coat, quartzite socks, cabochon sapphire eyes and holding a silver-gilt shovel. Engraved ФАБЕРЖЕ under right foot. [84]
Height 4½ inches
HCB colour plate 98   AKS colour plate XLVII

N2, N8 and N9, Madame Josiane Woolf, France.

N10 A PORTRAIT MODEL of the house boy (*dvornik*) who used to sweep out Fabergé's St Petersburg premises. The face in aventurine quartz with sapphire eyes, shirt in lapis-lazuli, breeches in grey Kalgan jasper, waistcoat in obsidian, white translucent quartz apron and obsidian boots and cap, to which is applied a pierced gold badge giving the address of the firm; 24 Morskaya, beneath, the word *dvornik* in Russian characters. He holds a gold broom. Engraved ФАБЕРЖЕ under right boot. [84]
Height 5 inches
HCB colour plate 97   AKS colour plate XLV

N1, N7 and N10, Mr John Cowdy, Northern Ireland.

N11 GIPSY WOMAN with a dark aventurine quartz face and hands, striated jasper skirt, purpurine kerchief, black Siberian jasper hair, calcite shoes, mottled green, quartz blouse and an extremely realistic Paisley shawl in figured red-brown jasper. The eyes are brilliant diamonds, the ear-rings and chain gold and the coins Nicholas II silver. This sculpture is a portrait model of Vara Panina, the celebrated gipsy, the extraordinary range and beauty of whose voice kept audiences entranced nightly at Moscow's Tzigane restaurant Yar in spite of her lack of beauty. When her love for a member of the Imperial Guard was unrequited, she dramatically took poison and died on the stage in front of him singing 'My heart is breaking'. [102]
Height 7 inches
AKS colour plate XLVI
A la Vieille Russie, New York.

N12 COSSACK (*cherkèss*) with a great-coat carved from slate, shirt with high collar of lapis-lazuli, and belt in opaque black-enamelled silver with a silver nielloed dagger attached. Wearing a long sash and hood in a pale grey composition with gold cord and tassels, black obsidian boots, fur hat in alabaster set with a turquoise and hands, face and beard in composition with cabochon sapphire eyes. Engraved under the feet: ФАБЕРЖЕ 1915.
Height 8¾ inches
HCB plate 99

N13 A STREET PEDLAR (*raznoschik*) with coat carved from a natural rock, white marble apron, slate boots, granite mittens, hat in black obsidian and lapis-lazuli, face in a composition with beard and hair in alabaster and cabochon sapphire eyes. Carrying a portable tea-urn in grey marble with a silver-gilt spigot and knop and a tray of brown banded jasper with three crystal-quartz tea glasses. He holds another tea glass, in smoky quartz simulating a full glass of tea and with four bread rings in coral hanging from a gold thread tied round one arm. Engraved under the feet: ФАБЕРЖЕ 1914.
Height 6¼ inches
HCB plate 99

N14 A figure of JOHN BULL wearing a pur-purine coat, white quartzite trousers and shirt, lapis-lazuli waistcoat, hat and boots in black jasper, the latter with mustard-coloured tops. Hair and face in aventurine quartz and set with faceted sapphire eyes. He wears a miniature bloodstone and gold revolving pendant seal and carries a gold cane under one arm, fully signed and bearing the initials HW. Commissioned by Queen Alexandra as a gift for the King.
Height 4¾ inches
Sir Charles Clore, London.

CASE O

O1 CORONATION EGG, presented to Alexandra Feodorovna by Nicholas II, dated 1897. This superb red gold Egg, enamelled translucent lime yellow on an engraved field, is enclosed by a green gold laurel leaf trellis, work cage mounted at each intersection by a yellow gold Imperial double-headed eagle enamelled opaque black, and set with a rose diamond. A large portrait diamond is set in the top of the egg within a cluster of ten brilliant diamonds; through the table of this stone, the monogram of the Empress is seen, the crowned 'A' described in rose diamonds, and the Russian 'F' in cabocohon rubies set in an opaque white enamel plaque. Another, smaller, portrait diamond is set within a cluster of rose diamonds at the end of the Egg, beneath which the date is inscribed on a similar plaque.

The surprise concealed inside this elaborate shell is an exact replica of the Imperial coach used in 1896, at the Coronation of Nicholas and Alexandra in Moscow. In yellow gold and strawberry coloured translucent enamel, the coach, one of the most splendid achievements of the goldsmith's art, is surmounted by the Imperial Crown in rose diamonds and six double-headed eagles on the roof; it is fitted with engraved rock crystal windows and platinum tyres, and is decorated with a diamond-set trellis in gold and an Imperial eagle in diamonds on either door. It is perfectly articulated in all its parts, even to the two steps which may be let down when the doors are opened, and the whole chassis is correctly slung. The interior is enamelled with pale blue curtains behind the upholstered seats and footstool, and a daintily painted ceiling with a turquoise-blue sconce and hook set in the centre. The meticulous chasing of this astonishing piece was carried out with the naked eye without even the aid of a loupe. George Stein, who made the coach while he was employed in Perchin's workshop, explains that at that time, when he was a young man of twenty-three, his sight was so good that he could easily detect a flaw in a diamond by simply holding it up to the light. He evidently spent about fifteen months on this model, paying many exploratory visits to the famous Coach Museum in St Petersburg before starting the work. His pay was considered lavish at the rate of 5 roubles (or 10 shillings) a day – days which were sometimes sixteen hours long; Stein only earned three roubles a day at Kortmann's, his previous place of employment, but the conditions were better there than at Fabergé's before the removal to new premises in 1900. The yellow and black shell of the Egg is a reference to the sumptuous Cloth of Gold robe worn by the Tsarina at her Coronation.

The name Wigström, Perchin's assistant, is roughly scratched on the inner surface of the shell. [101]

Height of egg 5 inches

Length of coach 3 $\frac{11}{16}$ inches

Signed MΠ   Gold mark, crossed anchors

HCB colour plate 58   AKS colour plate LXXIII

O2 LILIES OF THE VALLEY EGG, presented to the Dowager Empress Marie Feodorovna by Nicholas II, dated 5th April 1898. Gold Egg enamelled translucent rose on a *guilloché* field and supported on four dull green gold cabriolet legs composed of overlapping leaves veined with rose diamonds. The Egg is surmounted by a rose diamond and cabochon ruby Imperial Crown set with two bows and quartered by four lines of rose diamonds and decorated with lilies of the valley in pearls and rose diamonds, the stalks lightly engraved green gold and the leaves enamelled translucent green on gold. The 'surprise' consists of three oval miniatures of Nicholas II in military uniform, and the Grand Duchess Olga and Tatiana, his first two children, signed by Zehngraf within rose diamond borders which are drawn out of the top of the egg by means of a geared mechanism and spread into a fan when a gold-mounted pearl button at the side is turned; a turn in the opposite direction automatically folds and returns the miniatures back to the interior of the egg. The date is engraved on the reverse of the miniatures. [101]

Height (closed) 5 $\frac{15}{16}$ inches (extended) 7 $\frac{7}{8}$ inches

Signed MΠ   Gold mark, crossed anchors

O1 and O2, Wartski, London.

03

03 THE FIRST IMPERIAL EASTER EGG, presented to Marie Feodorovna by Alexander III, probable date 1884. This was the first of the Fabergé Imperial Easter Eggs, and the pleasure that it gave to both the Tsar, who presented it, and the Tsarina, who received it, established a custom which was to continue without interruption until the violent end of the Romanov dynasty.

The shell of the Egg is gold, enamelled opaque white, and polished to give the effect of a hen's egg. The two halves are held together by a bayonet fitting; when these are opened, a yellow gold yolk with a dull sandblasted surface is revealed. Inside this yolk, which opens in the same way as the shell, sits a yellow and white tinted gold hen as though in a nest. Each feather is most carefully engraved, and two cabochon ruby eyes are set in the head; the

beak and comb are in red gold. By lifting the head, the hen opens on a hinge at the tail. Originally, a diamond replica of the Imperial Crown was contained within the hen, and when this was opened, a tiny ruby pendant was found hanging inside.

Height of Egg 2½ inches
Length of hen 1⅜ inches
There are no marks at all on this egg.
AKS plates 313–316

04 RESURRECTION EGG, presented to Marie Feodorovna by Alexander III, made between 1885 and 1890. In the form of a monstrance, this Resurrection Egg is one of Fabergé's masterpieces; exquisitely made in the manner of the Italian Renaissance, it is essentially a jewel.

The three gold figures in the group are

naturalistically enamelled *en ronde bosse* with white drapery and lilac-coloured wings. The grass and the ground upon which the group is arranged are enamelled pale green and brown with yellow flecks, and this base is surrounded by a narrow belt of rose diamonds. The door of the Tomb is enamelled to simulate marble with a coral-coloured handle. The whole Resurrection scene is contained within a carved rock crystal Egg, the two hemispheres held together by a line of rose diamonds. The plinth supporting the Egg is enamelled translucent strawberry, green and opaque white with opaque black-painted enamel motifs, and opaque cerulean blue. The gold used is yellow, and the piece is set with eight brilliant diamonds in opaque black enamel collets; an Indian pearl is set on each of the four main panels of the base which is richly set with rose diamonds, and a large pearl serves as the shaft for this Egg.

Height 3⅞ inches   Signed МП
Gold mark crossed anchors
AKS plate 317

05 Red gold shaped miniature STRUT-FRAME, with domed top with an outer border of chased dull green gold acanthus running along an opalescent oyster enamelled path over engraving, applied with chased green gold leaves interrupted by red gold chased rosettes. The main area of the frame is enamelled translucent pink over *guilloché* sunrays and is overlaid with dull green gold chased swags and a garland of berried laurel with burnished red gold bows of ribbon. The circular aperture above is edged by half-pearls and contains painted portrait miniatures of the Grand Duchesses Marie and Anastasia in embroidered white dresses. The lower rectangular aperture is framed by an acanthus border and contains a miniature

04

05

painting of a nursing home in the country where the Grand Duchesses worked as Sisters. Both paintings are signed by Vassily Zuiev and dated 1916; the portraits with initials and landscape with his full name.
Height 7⅜ inches   Signed HW
Mr John S. Sheldon, London

06 Triptych IKON in the Byzantine style, in silver-gilt, richly set with emeralds, rubies, sapphires and pearls. Presented by the nobility of St Petersburg to Nicholas II and the Empress on November 3rd 1895, the occasion of the birth of their first child, the Grand Duchess Olga. It portrays their respective patron Saints, Nicholas, Alexandra and Olga, painted on silver in natural colours against a dark brown background. The outside is panelled with Russian birch finished in ivory, and is designed to represent a church steeple. The framework is finely chased and set with emeralds, rubies and sapphires. [83]
Height 10¼ inches   Signed MΠ
AKS plates 73, 74 and 75

07 Red and green gold COLUMN SURMOUNTED BY THE IMPERIAL EAGLE and supported upon four reeded bun feet. The column is chased with husks and berries and the base with a border of guilloche and foliate swags. An oval miniature likeness of Nicholas II, framed and crowned with brilliant and rose diamonds, hangs from the column.
Height 6¼ inches   Signed HW

06 and 07, A la Vieille Russie, New York.

08 TWILIGHT EGG, designed for either the Tsarina or the Dowager Empress, dated 1917. A gold Easter Egg encrusted with a mosaic of lapis-lazuli and conceived as a night-sky studded

07

with inalaid *paillons* cut as stars. In the front, a pair of pierced gold gates fashioned to resemble wrought iron, are supported on either side by carved lapis pilasters, the capitals of which are inlaid with gold. When opened, these gates, which are surmounted by a double-headed eagle and the Imperial Crown in gold, reveal a gold panel engraved with a garden view of Peterhof. The back of the Egg is set with a lapis Romanov eagle carved in relief beneath which the year 1917 is inlaid in engraved gold. Rose diamond and faceted moonstone clusters have been applied to the egg to act as push-piece and finial respectively. The interior is fitted with three gold loops clearly intended to secure a surprise which is now missing.

There is no evidence that the 1917 Eggs were ever completed, and the uncharacteristic jewels in their heavy claw settings, the engraved panel and the marks may well have been later additions to the original lapis lazuli body with its stars and date. Moonstones, normally cut *en cabochon*, with their special significance in this particular context, may well have been in Fabergé's mind, but they would then, one may assume, have been set flush with the body of the Egg as was the custom of the House. This fascinating object, with a Chinese provenance, made its appearance at an auction in Geneva in November 1976.

Mr Bainbridge has left an illuminating note on page 74 of his book based on the testimony of Fabergé's eldest son Eugenè:

Fabergé continued with the making of the two eggs for Easter 1917, but by the time Easter arrived the Tsar, with the Tsarina and their five children, were prisoners in the Alexander Palace, in Tsarkoe Selo, and it is to the everlasting shame of the Pro-

08   08

Ludwig II relived the drama of his ungracious idol's Götterdämmerung, may have provided the true inspiration for this undeniably romantic egg.

Despite the initials HW stamped on this Egg, it seems far more likely that it is in fact the product of Hölmstrom's jewellery workshop, as is certainly the case with Fabergé's other more lavish Mosaic Egg of 1916 (F5) which, curiously enough, also bears an unconvincing signature.

Height 5⅝ inches   Signed HW
Herr Fritz Attinger, Zürich.

09 Square red gold STRUT CLOCK with chased green gold acanthus border, enamelled translucent royal blue over a sunburst engraving, scattered with silver stars set with rose diamonds. The Roman numerals are painted black on a band of opalescent white enamel over engraved lines framed by an opaque white enamelled raised border. The centre of the clock is set with a piece of crystal frosted to give the impression of moonstone, carved in relief with the face of the man-in-the-moon within a border of half pearls. The hands emerge from behind this face and travel round the dial.

4 5/16 inches square   Signed HW

O10 PEACOCK EGG, presented to the Dowager Empress Marie Feodorovna by Nicholas II, dated 1908. This rock crystal Easter Egg in Louis XV taste, engraved with crowned monogram of Marie Feodorovna and the date, each within a border of scrolls, is supported on a silver-gilt scrolling base. Within the Egg a mechanical gold enamelled peacock, one of Fabergé's most ingenious creations, is perched in the branches of an engraved gold tree with flowers in enamel and precious stones. The Egg

visional Government that delivery of them was not allowed. Where they are today and what they were made of I have not been able to find out, but Eugenè Fabergé tells me that so far as his memory goes, one of them was in Karelian birch.

A water-colour design for an Easter Egg in the form of a rotary clock incorporating a globe scattered with stars, signed *C. Fabergé* and dated 1917, is illustrated in AKS plate 386, indi-

cating that this particular theme was exercising his imagination at the time. That this Egg should symbolise the twilight of the Romanovs may seem to us today a little far fetched, but it would have been seen as singularly appropriate by the Imperial couple, especially the Tsarina, who regarded herself and her spouse as little short of holy objects. Perhaps the starry night sky painted above the Throne Room in the Bavarian alpine retreat of Neuschwanstein in the early 1880s, under which the eccentric

falls into two halves, each with a heavily chased silver-gilt rococo mount, when opened at the top by means of a clasp. The peacock, when lifted from the branches, wound up and placed on a flat surface, struts proudly about, placing one leg carefully before the other, moving its head and, at intervals, spreading and closing its vari-coloured enamel tail. [39]

Eugène Fabergé has written in a letter dated March 19th 1952:

Of the many clever craftsmen I would single out Dorofeev, a self-taught mechanic. It was he who made the mechanical peacock for a rock crystal egg. It took him three years to make it.

Height of egg 6 inches
Length of peacock 4¾ inches
Signed HW
HCB plate 65   AKS plates 356 and 357

O11 SHIP'S CHRONOMETER in red gold and chocolate-coloured agate. The movement, by Brinkman, London, is balanced on gimbels and the hinged cover opens by means of a button, with glazed interior. The main opening, also hinged, locks with a small gold key, the keyhole being in an opaque white enamelled gold disc on the front, inscribed in black enamel *C. Fabergé, St Petersburg*. Two gold free-swinging handles are on the sides of this simply designed scientific instrument and the key for the movement is accommodated inside. [104]
Height 4 inches   Signed HW

O12 Dark grey dappled agate oval SNUFF-BOX mounted in red gold chased with green gold laurel and set with a briolet-cut diamond thumb-piece. The hinged cover is emblazoned with a green gold Imperial Romanov Eagle,

partly tinted red and enamelled opaque black with painted enamel ribbon and shields.
Length 3⅛ inches   Signed AH
Gold mark crossed anchors
AKS plate 129

O13 Ostrich-feather FAN with engraved rock crystal handle, with a red gold circular mount enamelled translucent pink over a *moiré* ground with opaque white borders, set with rose diamonds and fitted with a small looking-glass on one side enabling the wearer discreetly to observe those around her.

Length of handle 7 inches   Signed HW
AKS plates 182 and 183

O14 Coronation PRESENTATION BOX in red gold, enamelled translucent chartreuse yellow on sunray and wave-patterned grounds, with chased green gold husk borders, the cover mounted with a brilliant diamond-set trellis with opaque black-enamelled Romanov double-headed eagles and, at the centre, the Imperial cypher of Nicholas II within an oval crowned border, all in brilliant diamonds,

O13

applied to a panel engraved with a sunray and enamelled opalescent oyster. This sumptuous box was given by the Tsarina to her husband on Easter Day 1897, the day she received the Coronation Egg (O1). [81]
Length 3⅝ inches   Signed АН
Gold mark crossed anchors
АKS colour plate I

O13 and O14 Forbes Magazine collection, New York.

O15 Oval engraved and reeded red gold BOX, the sides enamelled opalescent oyster with chased green gold acanthus borders framing articulated painted ivory puppets; one a young girl set in the cover, another a young man set in the base, both against dull black oxidised silver backgrounds. When the box is moved, the figures appear to dance realistically. This box, known as the Opera Box, was designed to commemorate a gala performance of Tchaikovsky's opera 'The Queen of Spades'; the two dancers depict characters from the pastorial interlude in the second act.
Length 2⅓ inches   Signed НW
АKS colour plates LX and LXI

O16 Pair of red gold OPERA GLASSES, chased with rococo scrolling and reserved with granulated areas, set with rubies, rose diamonds and two brilliants.
Length 4 inches   Signed МП
Mr and Mrs Bing Crosby, California.

O17 Circular matt and granulated gold DISH *repoussé* with a swirling *rocaille* design of waves, scrolls, ribbons and flowers set with brilliant and rose diamonds, rubies and sapphires.
Diameter 4¼ inches   Signed ES
Gold marks 72 and crossed anchors

016

O18 SPRAY OF BUTTERCUPS, modelled in gold and finely chased, with buds and flowerheads set with brilliant diamonds and enamelled translucent pale yellow in a rock crystal pot.
Height 6 inches   No marks

O19 Rectangular PHOTOGRAPH FRAME in red gold chased with an acanthus border and with two green gold leaf and berry sprays applied to a field of opalescent oyster enamel over a sunray ground. The oval aperture is rimmed by rose diamonds. It is supported on a reeded and chased dull yellow gold easel with a green gold foliate swag, red gold bow knot and three beaded cone feet. [102]
Height 5⅞ inches   Signed КФ

O17 to O19, Madame Josiane Woolf, France.

O20 Miniature replica of a Louis XVI dropfront SECRETAIRE (*secrétaire a abbatant*) in dark brown agate simulating veneered wood, decorated with reeded columns, rosettes, swags, trophies and borders in engraved and chased red, green and yellow gold. Two oval and four rectangular plaques enamelled opales-

99

cent warm sepia over engraving and painted with musical and military trophies imitate Sèvres porcelain panels. The top, set with a rock crystal panel engraved with scrolls, acts as the hinged cover to a compartment. [104] Height 5¼ inches   Signed МП HCB colour plate 38

021 Mechanical SEDAN CHAIR in engraved red gold with green gold acanthus borders, enamelled translucent yellow over a ground engraved with Romanov double-headed eagles within trails of leaves. The windows and roof are set with bevelled rock crystal panels. A miniature gold figure of Catherine the Great in her Imperial ermine cloak, enamelled in natural translucent colours and wearing a rose diamond crown and Order, is seated inside. The chair is borne along by two scarlet-coated blackamoors in gold and enamel who walk naturalistically when the clockwork mechanism is wound with a small gold key. [121] Overall length 3⅛ inches   Gold mark 72 Signed HW AKS colour plate LIII and plate 286

022 A pair of LOVING CUPS in yellow, red, green and white golds, the flat sided flared stems are ribbed laterally, each of the four sides in a different colour, and the circular bowls patterned with diamond-shaped areas similarly varied in colour, each engraved in imitation of a peacock feather. A bayonet fitting enables the cups to be joined together forming a globe.

OPPOSITE Left 01   Right 02
OVERLEAF Left MI   Middle NII   Right 019

Height 3 $\frac{9}{16}$ inches   Signed МП
Gold mark crossed anchors
AKS colour plate XXIX

020, 021 and 022 Sir Charles Clore, London.

023 EASTER EGG carved in a banded agate and
mounted with a gold bezel enamelled opaque
white and reserved with gold lettering which
reads:

*Comme j'aime quand j'aime, j'aime qu'on
m'aime*

The hinged cover is mounted with a chased
thumb-piece set with a demantoid garnet and
two rose diamonds.
Height 2 $\frac{3}{8}$ inches   Signed МП

024 PRESENTATION BOX in coloured golds with
chased matt gold mounts, designed to celebrate the Declaration of Bulgarian Inde-
pendance on October 5th 1908 for Ferdinand,
who was proclaimed Tsar on that day. The
miniature portrait of the Monarch on the
cover, signed by Zehngraf, is set within a
frame of brilliant diamonds surmounted by
the Bulgarian crown and *fleur de lis* motifs are
repeated at the four corners. The portrait is
applied to a sunburst panel of translucent
enamel representing a cloth of gold within an
elaborate border of opalescent oyster enamel
with boldly chased gold scrolling floral strapwork. The sides of the box are enamelled with
the same oyster, enlivened by the *moiré*

OVERLEAF   *Above* 024   *Below* 025   *Right* P13
OPPOSITE   *Left* 011   *Right* 020

023

guilloché ground and when moved a hint of
flame glints beneath the surface.
    The late H. C. Bainbridge has reported in his
book *Twice Seven* (Routledge 1933) a con-
versation with Ferdinand, popularly known as
Foxy Ferdie: ' "My dear Monsieur Fabergé,
I wish you were in Bulgaria, I should make you
my Minister" and the reply, "No, no Your
Majesty, not politics, I beg of you, of such
things I am ignorant – but Minister of the
Goldsmith's Art, why yes Sire, if you will
it." ' [103]
Length 3 $\frac{5}{16}$ inches   Gold mark 72
Signed HW

025 Red gold CIGARETTE BOX, reserved with
panels enamelled translucent emerald green
over *moiré* engraving edged with opaque white
enamelled lines and pellets, the main outer
borders in granulated yellow gold overlaid
with chased green gold leaves and red gold
rosettes and ribbons. [103]
Length 3 $\frac{5}{8}$ inches   Signed HW   Gold mark 72

026 SNUFF-BOX of rectangular canted form,
in engraved yellow gold decorated with two
views of Chatsworth painted above and below
in warm sepia enamel, the sides with four
decorative panels with twisted foliate and
floral trails in the same technique. Edged with
fine opaque white enamel lines, the broad
borders are of granulated gold enriched with
leaf and berry motifs in translucent emerald
and strawberry enamel. This box, in Louis
XVI taste, was commissioned by the then Duke
of Devonshire. [82]
Length 2 $\frac{1}{2}$ inches   Signed HW
Gold mark 72
AKS plates 123–127
The Duke of Devonshire and the Trustees of
the Chatsworth Settlement.

Underside of 026

027 DIAMOND TRELLIS EGG, presented to Marie Feodorovna by Alexander III, probable date 1892. Carved in bowenite and encased in a fine and gently undulating trellis of rose diamonds, the pale yellow-green colour of the serpentine with its opalescent finish adds to the overall delicacy of this elegant object by Fabergé's chief jeweller. The Easter Egg is hinged and set at the top with a large rose diamond.

Height 4¼ inches
Signed AH
Gold mark crossed anchors
AKS colour plate LXX

027

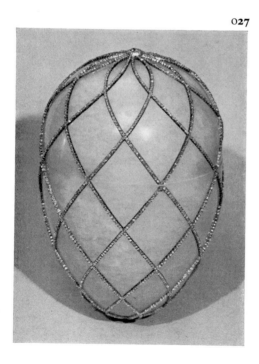

028 EGG WITH REVOLVING MINIATURES, presented to Alexandra Feodorovna by Nicholas II, probable date 1896. The two halves of this rock crystal egg are held together by a narrow rose diamond and translucent emerald green enamelled gold mount, culminating at the top with an elaborately-set Siberian emerald weighing 27 carats, cabochon and pointed. The Egg is supported on a circular rock crystal plinth decorated with *champlevé* enamel of various colours and richly set with rose diamonds; the monograms of the Tsarina, as the Princess Alix of Hesse-Darmstadt before her marriage, and as Alexandra Feodorovna, Empress of Russia, each surmounted by their respective crown, appear as separate continuous formal patterns encircling this plinth. Twelve miniature paintings signed by Zehngraf, framed in chased gold guilloche, revolve round a fluted gold shaft which passes through the centre of the Egg when the cabochon emerald in the top is depressed and turned. The miniatures show Royal Residences in Germany, England and Russia associated with the life of the Tsarina and include views of various palaces in and around Darmstadt and Coburg in Germany, Windsor Castle, Osborne House and Balmoral in Great Britain and the Alexander, Anitchkov and Winter Palaces in Russia.

Height 9¾ inches   Signed MΠ
Gold mark crossed anchors
AKS plates 327–329
In the Lilian Thomas Pratt collection of the Virginia Museum of Fine Arts.

029 Double-opening CIGARETTE CASE, in yellow gold enamelled opalescent rose on both sides over a *moiré* ground, bordered by translucent emerald enamel leaves on granulated red gold paths between lines of opaque white

028

Rosenau, Coburg and Tsarskoe Selo   (detail) 028

translucent blue over *guilloché* ground with the year 2456 (1913) reserved on a band from which hangs the medallion painted in enamel with two pigs. The majority of the medals presented bore only a single pig, but those who were born in the same year as the Queen received a medal with two pigs. The wording on the reverse of the medallion translates 'Don't forget to regard the pig'.

Width $1\frac{1}{8}$ inches   Height $3\frac{7}{16}$ inches
Diameter of pendant $1\frac{1}{16}$ inches
Signed ФАБЕРЖЕ

029 and 030, Mr Douglas A. Latchford, Bangkok.

030

enamel and with a rose diamond push-piece. Made for King Chulalongkorn, Rama VI of Siam.

Length $3\frac{1}{16}$ inches   Signed HW
Gold mark 72

030   MEDAL struck to celebrate the Year of the Pig, presented on the occasion of the 50th birthday of Queen Sawabhapongse, the wife of King Chulalongkorn, Rama VI of Siam. The ribbon, carried out in gold, is enamelled

CASE P

P1 Rectangular yellow gold MINIATURE FRAME with chased red gold mounts, composed of two fluted Siberian jade columns at either side joined by a pointed arch and standing upon a base enamelled translucent green, which is in turn supported upon two stud feet. The area surrounding the rectangular aperture, enamelled translucent oyster over a wavy *guilloché* ground, is overlaid above with a crisply chased foliate and floral garland in dull green gold with burnished red gold ribbon, and below with a spray of leaves set with a rose diamond. [82]
Height 4⅛ inches   Signed K. ФАБЕРЖЕ
Mr and Mrs E. Amirkhanian, Tehran.

P2 GYPSOPHILA, with flowers in translucent green enamel with rose diamond centres, engraved dull green gold stalks, moss in yellow and red gold in a carved nephrite jar. Formerly in the collection of Queen Olga of Greece.
Height 7 inches   No marks
AKS plate 295

P3 Large Siberian jade DISH mounted with two engraved yellow gold handles chased with scrolling in Louis XV style, lavishly set with rose diamonds and enamelled translucent strawberry over a *guilloché* ground.
Overall width 17½ inches   Signed MП
Gold mark crossed anchors
HCB plate 19   AKS plate 279

P2

P4 Nephrite FREEDOM BOX of tubular form, enriched with scrolling borders, laurel mounts, festoons and swags in chased red and green golds. It is supported upon three ball feet and

the fluted cover is surmounted by a partly burnished matt yellow gold Imperial Eagle.
Height 8¾ inches   Signed MП
Gold mark crossed anchors
HCB plate 8   AKS plate 275

P2, P3 and P4, Lady Zia Wernher, Luton Hoo.

P5 Siberian jade 'KOVSH' designed as a swan, the head set with two cabochon rubies, and neck with carefully chased and engraved feathers in green and red golds, the tail, which serves as the handle, reeded in the same golds framing a gold five rouble piece of 1898 partly enamelled translucent strawberry.
Length 4 inches   Signed HW
Gold mark 72
Bentley, London.

P6 Carved nephrite EGG with a red and green gold bezel chased with a border of Vitruvian scrolls. The thumb-piece is set with a cabochon garnet and two rose diamonds. When opened, two hinged panels are revealed which act as covers for the two halves.
Height 4 1/16 inches   Signed MП
Gold mark crossed anchors

P7 Nephrite CHIMING CLOCK applied with chased yellow gold motifs in Empire taste.
Height 5½ inches   Signed HW
AKS plate 145

P6

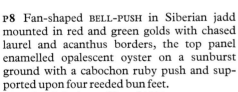

P5

P9 Siberian jade TAZZA, the circular dish is supported by two addorsed nude girls, carved in the manner of Maillol, acting as caryatids with cascades of water flowing over the rims of two pitchers between them, suggesting 'La Source' as subject. The silver-gilt base is reeded and stands upon four chased and granulated feet. An early example (before 1896), of an 'art work'.
Height 8½ inches   Signed MΠ
Silver mark crossed anchors

P7

P8 Fan-shaped BELL-PUSH in Siberian jadd mounted in red and green golds with chased laurel and acanthus borders, the top panel enamelled opalescent oyster on a sunburst ground with a cabochon ruby push and supported upon four reeded bun feet.
Length 2 9/16 inches   Signed MΠ
AKS plate 177

P9

P10 Rectangular reeded and engraved red gold TABLE BOX mounted *en cage*, the borders enamelled opaque white with translucent emerald leaves over engraved veining. The hinged cover, base and sides are set with rectangular panels of thinly carved Siberian jade and the box stands on four gold bun feet.
[122]
Length 3¾ inches   Signed MΠ
Gold mark crossed anchors
Wartski, London.

P11 Circular Siberian jade DISH, the high surrounding wall with a reeded and engraved red gold mount enamelled opaque white and set with eight faceted sapphires.
Diameter 5 inches   Signed HW

P12 Carved Siberian jade shallow DISH in Renaissance style, of rectangular form with gently curved ends. The red gold chased handles are reserved with fields of granulated yellow gold and are composed of an elaborate system of scrolls enamelled translucent scarlet and pale green on *guilloché* backgrounds and opaque black and white. To give yet another dimension to this already sumptuous object, rivers of rose diamonds and large single stones in raised collets serve to light up and punctuate this splendid example of St Petersburg work. It is cradled in an engraved gold strapwork frame. It was presented to Queen Wilhelmina of the Netherlands on the occasion of the Royal Dutch Wedding in 1901 by the Dutch colony living in St Petersburg. [82]
Length 13⅝ inches   Signed MΠ
Reproduced in colour in *The Connoisseur* of June 1962.

P13 PARASOL HANDLE, designed as a nephrite carving of a frog with rose diamond eyes set in gold, climbing a tubular column enamelled translucent emerald green over *moiré* en-

graving, mounted at its base with a chased red and green foliate border within bands of opaque white enamel. [103]
Height 4½ inches   Signed HW

P14 Siberian nephrite CUP with a chased gold handle enamelled *champlevé* in translucent strawberry on a *guilloché* background and set with rose diamonds. This was a favourite early design of Erik Kollin, and although this piece is unsigned, presumably for lack of a suitable place for stamping, it is almost certainly from his hand. Another example, in bowenite, is illustrated in AKS colour plate XXX.
Height 1⅝ inches   No marks
AKS colour plate XV

P15 Siberian jade PHOTOGRAPH FRAME the circular pearl-bordered aperture is surrounded by a chased garland of roses in four colours of gold. It is surmounted by a bow knot of gold ribbon which threads through the flowers to descend in two streams culminating in tassels set with rose diamonds and two cabochon rubies.
Height 4¼ inches   Signed ЯА

P16 Siberian jade CIGAR BOX composed of six rectangular panels mounted *en cage* in chased gold enamelled *champlevé* translucent strawberry over engraving reserved with gold foliate

paillons. Standing on four feet, the top forming a hinged lid, the angles are embossed with three acanthus quatrefoils.
Length 6⅝ inches   Signed MΠ
Gold mark crossed anchors
AKS plate 178
Mr Nicholas Fairbairn, QC, MP, Fordell.

P17 Siberian jade hinged WRITING-BLOCK, the border in red gold chased with dull green gold acanthus, embellished with an elaborate festoon composed of flowers chased in four colours of gold, sprays and bow-knots, set with three cabochon rubies and a brilliant diamond. The block is set on a dark palisander wood base.
Length of jade block 6¾ inches
Signed HW
HCB plate 45

P18 MAGNIFYING GLASS in red gold with chased green gold laurel and a reeded nephrithe andle.
Length 6⅝ inches   Signed MΠ
Gold mark crossed anchors

P17 and P18 Mr John S. Sheldon, London.

P19 Gold and nephrite PEN-REST with red gold mounts, one of which is fluted and set with a cabochon ruby.
Length 1 11/16 inches   No marks
Madame Josiane Woolf, France.

P21

P20 Red gold HAND SEAL, composed of a nephrite sphere with a crown rose diamond set in the top supported by three chased yellow gold dolphins set with cabochon ruby eyes, resting on a circular nephrite platform. Above and below are borders of alternating pellets of opaque white and translucent strawberry enamel, the latter over engraved backgrounds, The matrix is of pale grey chalcedony.
Height $2\frac{3}{16}$ inches   Signed МП

P21 CROCHET HOOK in nephrite, with collar enamelled opalescent oyster over a wave patterned field, mounted in chased red and green gold, set with rose diamonds and with a carved nephrite pineapple knop.
Length $10\frac{5}{16}$ inches   Signed HW
AKS plate 224

P22 Siberian jade RULER, mounted with chased yellow and red gold scrolling in rococo taste relieved with flowerheads.
Length $7\frac{7}{8}$ inches   No marks

P23 PEN HOLDER, with a reeded nephrite handle and shaft enamelled translucent scarlet over matching engraving, bounded by red gold mounts decorated with chased green bands of laurel. A moonstone thumb-piece slides along the barrel and allows the mount holding the nib to appear and retract. [122]
Length retracted $7\frac{15}{16}$ inches   Signed AR
This unidentified Fabergé workmaster, possibly active in Odessa or Kiev, is only known by his initials. See AKS page 128.
Wartski, London.

P24 Nephrite ELEPHANT with cabochon ruby eyes and diamonds set in the tip of the trunk.
Length $2\frac{1}{2}$ inches
AKS colour plate XXXIV

P25 An amusing carving of a FROG in nephrite, set with rose diamond eyes, with its front legs thrust into its mouth and one back leg jerked to one side.
Height 1 inch

P26 Nephrite carving of a crouching SQUIRREL with rose diamond eyes set in gold, nibbling at a nut.
Height $1\frac{7}{8}$ inches

CASE Q

Q1 HEAD ORNAMENT in brilliant diamonds, composed of two sprays of *Aucuba variegata*, the stalks are engraved red gold, leaves in a rubbed-over silver setting, pierced to suggest veining, backed in gold.
Each spray, which is made in two parts, measures $7\frac{1}{2}$ inches in length.
Signed КФ
AKS plate 219

Q2 Set of six red gold-mounted DRESS BUTTONS, each bordered with chased dull green gold leaves and enamelled opalescent oyster over a sunray *guilloché* ground, set with a faceted ruby in the centre.
Diameter of each button $\frac{5}{8}$ inch
Signed HW

Q3 FLAMINGO standing upon one leg in chased dull green gold, the body composed of a single baroque pearl, with feathers and neck of massed rose diamonds and the head with cabochon ruby eyes set in gold, the half-opened beak enamelled a deep coral with dark brown tip and marking. The feet are webbed and the bird stands on one leg, on an oval bowenite base. [123]
Height $4\frac{5}{16}$ inches   No marks

Q1

Q6

Q4

Q5

Q4 EVENING BAG in green gold mesh, the red gold frame set with *calibré* sapphires and decorated with chased green gold laurel swags and red gold ribbons.
Width of frame 6½ inches
Signed K. ФАБЕРЖЕ
Mrs Laurel Albertini, Ibiza.

Q5 Chased and granulated yellow gold TORQUE with two lion heads and a twisted shaft, a faithful replica of a jewel from the Scythian Treasure.
Width 2⅞ inches   Signed EK
AKS plate 217

Q6 Gold FUR CLASP, the two octagonal panels enamelled translucent pale blue over engraved grounds and overlaid with a rose diamond-set trellis; the borders in green and red golds, chased with laurel and flowerheads within opaque white-enamelled lines. The centre of each panel is set with a sherry-coloured citrine within a frame of rose diamonds.
Length (extended) 5½ inches   Signed HW

Q7 Red gold-mounted oval PENDANT enamelled overall opalescent oyster on a sun-in-splendour *guilloché* ground, overlaid by a flower motif set with rose diamonds, a ruby drop and a cabochon sapphire. Suspended from a rose diamond-set loop, the jewel accommodates a miniature frame either side of the interior.
Overall height 1¾ inches   Signed МП
Lady Solti, London.

Q8 Diamond-shaped BROOCH in dull green gold enamelled translucent blue over an engine-turned ground and applied with a silver *fleur-de-lis* set with brilliant and rose diamonds.
Height 7¼ inches   Signed OP
Gold mark St George and dragon

Q9 DRESS WATCH in yellow gold, the back enamelled opalescent oyster with a hint of flame over a wavy sunburst engraving, edged by rose diamonds within white opaque enamelled lines with, at the centre, an embossed dull green gold rosette on a granu-

Q9

Q14

three pinned pearls on twin gold scrolls.
Length 1¾ inches   Signed МП
Gold mark crossed anchors

Q11 Gold BROOCH in the form of a rococo
cartouche, enamelled translucent blue over a
guilloché sunburst, the centre set with a brilliant diamond. The borders are composed of
three principal scrolls linked by three smaller
scrolls with chased gold and rose diamonds.
Height 1⅛ inches   Signed КФ
Gold mark St George and dragon
Dr Anita Katz, Ph.D., Syracuse, N.Y.

Q12 Red gold BROOCH, composed of a horse
shoe enamelled translucent pale blue over an
engraved ground with a brilliant diamond
trefoil set in silver and gold.
Height 15/16 inch   Signed КФ

Q13 Rectangular moss-agate BROOCH with
canted corners, mounted in gold and silver and
set with rose diamonds.
Length 1 1/16 inches   No marks
AKS colour plate XXXI

Q10

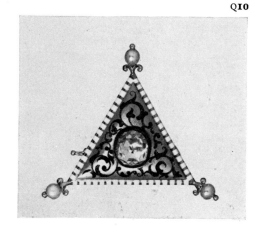

lated ground, encircled by another line of
white enamel. The reverse of this slim watch
shows an open dial framed in matching opalescent enamel over engraving and the bow is
enamelled *champlevé* in opaque white.

The movement is of Geneva manufacture
and the watch appears to be the only recorded
example by Fabergé.
Diameter of watch itself 1¾ inches
Signed HW   Gold mark 72

Q10 Triangular dull yellow gold *bombé*
BROOCH in Renaissance style, enamelled
champlevé with translucent scarlet scrolling
over engraving, bordered by rods of curved
section enamelled with opaque white interrupted by reserved gold divisions giving the
effect of stripes. The centre is set with a large
crown rose diamond and at the outer corners

Q14 Rectangular Russian aquamarine with
canted corners, mounted as a BROOCH-
PENDANT in a broad red gold frame set with
brilliant and rose cut diamonds following the
contour of the stone, and composed of inner
and outer borders connected by a rising open-
work trellis of intersecting zig-zags.
Length 1 9/16 inches   Signed HW
Gold mark crossed anchors

Q15 A PENDANT composed of an irregularly
carved piece of lapis-lazuli with a yellow
gold wishbone mount and ring.
Overall length 2⅛ inches
Signed КФ

Q16 Red gold BROOCH composed of a single
brilliant drop diamond suspended from a
scrolling framework set with *calibré* rubies.
Height 1 3/16 inches   Signed КФ
Madame Josiane Woolf, France.

114

Q17 A red gold link NECKLET, with seven mauve sapphires at intervals within green gold collets, framed by opalescent oyster enamel over a *guilloché* ground.
Length 8⅜ inches   Signed KФ

Q18 An unusual engraved gold miniature EASTER EGG enamelled in translucent stripes of pale green, cinnamon and rose over *guilloché* ground, the base culminating in a heart-shaped Mecca stone. [123] Another EGG carved as a conventionalized bird in purpurine with rose diamond eyes.
Length ¾ inch and ⅟₁₆ inch   Both signed KФ
AKS enamelled Egg, plate 215

Q19 Yellow gold hoop RING of a chequered design, set alternately with half pearls and rectangles enamelled translucent pale blue over engraved horizontal lines.
Width ¼ inch   Signed BA
Gold mark crossed anchors
AKS colour plate XXXI

Q20 Silver CIGARETTE-HOLDER, enamelled pale lilac over an engraved background, with a red gold mount with chased green gold laurel at either end of an amber mouthpiece.
Length 4⅝ inches   Signed KФ

Q18, Q19 and Q20, Mrs A. Kenneth Snowman, London.

Q21 Three miniature EASTER EGGS, one in platinum set with three rings of rose diamonds and one brilliant diamond, another also in platinum encircled by a broad grille of rose diamonds, and a gold Egg enamelled translucent strawberry over a *guilloché* ground and set with a brilliant diamond. The platinum

Eggs are unsigned but the third is signed A✶H
Overall length of both platinum Eggs 1 inch
Length of enamelled Egg ⅟₁₆ inch
AKS first Egg, plate 215
Mrs Harriette Snowman, London.

Q22

Q22 Pair of yellow gold CUFF LINKS of *bombé* form, enamelled in opalescent tones of apricot to pink on sunray backgrounds, with rose diamond borders and brilliant diamond centres.
Diameter ½ inch   Signed HW
AKS plate 220
Mr A. Kenneth Snowman, London.

Q23 Seven miniature EASTER EGGS in gold all set with rose diamonds, five enamelled in translucent colours and two in nephrite with the addition of rubies.
Lengths ranging from ⅝ to ⅞ inch
Five signed
Yellow egg with double band of diamonds signed EK.
Nephrite Egg with snake unsigned

Q24 Siberian jade NECKLACE linked by reeded gold rings joined by circles set on both sides with rose diamonds in silver. A diamond-shaped jade pendant, applied with a foliate spray and an arrow in rose and brilliant dia-

monds and two faceted rubies, hangs from the centre of the necklace.
Overall length 11⅝ inches   Signed MП

Q25 Rectangular silver BUCKLE with rounded corners, mounted in engraved red gold and enamelled translucent pale shrimp with four foliate mounts chased and engraved in dull green gold, each with a pink gold rosette.
Length 2¾ inches   Signed HW

Q26 Banded brown agate SWIVEL-SEAL, the stone a Sassanian dome intaglio seal engraved with two stags. The silver shank, authentically fashioned with ringed shoulders in imitation of the Old Persian manner of 400–500 AD, is the work of Erik Kollin who specialized in pastiches of this sort and was also known for his copies of jewels from the Scythian Treasure.
Height 1½ inches   Signed EK
Silver mark crossed anchors

Q26

CASE R

R1 Rectangular bowenite miniature STRUT FRAME, applied with a rococo cartouche boldly chased in yellow gold enamelled translucent rust over an engraved sun-in-splendour ground. Three flowers with leaves are composed of rose diamonds which are also used to enrich the elaborate scrolling border. The oval aperture is framed by half-pearls set in red gold.
Height 5½ inches   Signed МП
Gold mark crossed anchors

R2 Rectangular red gold STRUT CLOCK with green gold acanthus border, enamelled with broad stripes of translucent poppy red over engraved lines and with bouquets of roses and narrower stripes enamelled pale translucent green over engraved lines and laurel, each stripe bordered with opaque white enamel. The plain dial is edged by half-pearls and fitted with red gold pierced hands. [121]
Height 6 1/16 inches   Signed HW
Mr and Mrs Nigel Broackes

R3 Chased and engraved red gold MINIATURE FRAME designed as a Shield of David enamelled opalescent oyster and translucent pink over *guilloché* backgrounds. The circular aperture is bordered by half-pearls.
Height 3 inches   Signed МП
Gold mark crossed anchors

R4

R4 Pair of engraved TAPER-STICKS mounted in red and green gold with chased acanthus borders and rock crystal drip-plates, enamelled translucent royal blue and yellow in stripes, the Rothschild racing colours.
Height 2¾ inches   Signed HW
AKS plate 40

R5 Trefoil PERPETUAL CALENDAR in red gold, enamelled translucent pale rose over wavy sunburst engraving with painted sepia trails of twigs, the whole bordered by an opaque white enamelled line and with gold bow knots set with rose diamonds. The three circular apertures for the day, date and month, printed on ribbed silk, are rimmed with rose diamonds.
Height 3 1/16 inches   Signed K. ФАБЕРЖЕ

R6 Silver and silver-gilt BEZIQUE MARKER of rococo design enamelled translucent steel-grey over a *guilloché* ground which appears as pale lilac when moved, with hinged scoring panels enamelled opalescent oyster over engraved bars.
Length 4 3/16 inches   Signed МП
Silver mark crossed anchors

R7 Seated BEAR in obsidian, with rose diamond eyes set in gold.
Height 2⅞ inches
HCB plate 81

R4 to R7, Lady Zia Wernher, Luton Hoo.

R8 Gold HAND SEAL enamelled translucent blue over a *moiré guilloché* ground, the flared base in opalescent oyster over an identical ground with borders chased with Vitruvian scrolls. The matrix in grey-blue chalcedony.
Height 3⅜ inches   No marks

R9 Square gold TABLE CLOCK with borders of chased acanthus and opaque white enamel,

116

the main area enamelled opalescent peach painted with simulated moss-agate motifs over a sunray *guilloché* ground. The rose diamond-set numerals are applied to reserved concentric circles of opalescent white enamel over engraved backgrounds framed by chased foliate trails.

3½ inches square   Signed HW
Mr and Mrs J. Bloom, Johannesburg.

R10   Rectangular STRUT CLOCK in red gold with a chased green gold acanthus border, enamelled pale green against an engraved *moiré* ground with painted enamel sepia swags, garlands and bows. The broad border is enamelled a pale shade of translucent yellow-gold over a pattern of parallel lines and the dial similarly enamelled on a sunburst field; both embellished with painted sepia enamel foliate motifs. The dial is set within a border of half-pearls with pierced gold hands.

Height 6⅞ inches   Signed HW
AKS colour plate XXVI

R11   CIGAR BOX in red and green ribbed gold with a plain thumb-piece without jewels.

Length 5¾ inches   Signed К. ФАБЕРЖЕ
AKS plate 135

R11

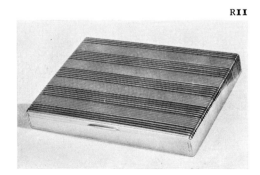

R12   Green gold CIGARETTE CASE engraved with two reeded and two barley-patterned bands, decorated with two borders of *champlevé* opaque white enamel in Greek key pattern, with a thumb-piece set with rose diamonds.

Length 3⅝ inches   Signed HW

R13

R13   Red gold CIGARETTE CASE, embossed with an all-over pattern of scallops, with a tinder attachment and match compartment, mounted with a thumb-piece set with a cabochon sapphire.

Length 3 13/16 inches   Signed GN
Gold mark crossed anchors
HCB plate 106

R14   Red gold CIGARETTE CASE of oval section, enamelled opaque white with engraved green gold intersecting trails of foliage and a rose diamond thumb-piece. This case bears the

gold mark L.Y.T. in Russian characters. Immediately after the Revolution, Fabergé's premises were taken over by an organisation known as the Leningradskoe Yuvelirnoe Tovarishchestvo (Leningrad Jewellery Brotherhood). This Brotherhood (at the early idealistic stage it may well have resembled a genuine Trade Union) inherited a number of completed and unfinished Fabergé objects, and these, together with pieces by other contemporary goldsmiths and silversmiths, they stamped with their own mark Л.Ю.Т. It is illustrated in AKS plate 405.

Length 3½ inches   Signed HW
Gold mark LYT
AKS plate 93

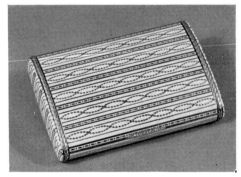

R14

R15   Unusually slim CIGARETTE BOX in reeded red and green golds forming a pattern of isosceles triangles, mounted with a rose diamond thumb-piece. This very chic object must be one of Fabergé's last designs in this genre.

Length 3¾ inches   Signed A★H

R17

R16 Engine-turned green and reeded red gold CIGARETTE BOX with inlaid opaque white enamelled lines and mounted with a rose diamond thumb-piece.
Length 3 7/16 inches   Signed A★H

R15 and R16, Bentley, London.

R17 Plaited double-opening CIGARETTE CASE composed of strips of red gold, platinum and green gold deeply chased with laurel and set with a brilliant diamond push-piece. An interesting forerunner of a design later to be widely exploited by the leading Paris goldsmiths.
Length 3½ inches   Signed A★H
Goldmark 72
Mr Robert Strauss, London.

R18 Red gold CIGARETTE CASE engraved with winged horses, griffins and swans, a winged female figure, scrolls and foliage in Empire taste; set with a cabochon sapphire push-piece.
Length 3½ inches   Signed MΠ
Wartski, London.

R19 Red gold MATCH CASE engraved with two swans and scrolls *en suite* with the previous exhibit but by a different workmaster. Set with a cabochon sapphire push-piece.
Length 1¾ inches   Signed A★H
S. J. Phillips, London.

R20 Miniature reeded CIGARETTE BOX in green and red golds with match compartment and

R18

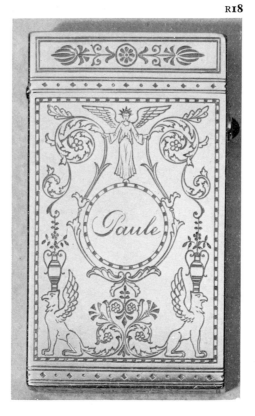

tinder attachment and mounted with a thumb-piece set with a cabochon sapphire. Shown in its original fitted holly wood box.
Length 3 inches   Signed A★H
M. et Mme Peter Zervudachi, Vevey.

R21 Silver-gilt octagonal TABLE CLOCK, with a reeded border, supported on four ball feet, enamelled opalescent oyster over a rayed ground applied with chased green gold trails of leaves and berries and swags with red gold ties and set with rose diamonds. The hands are of pierced red gold.
Width 3 11/16 inches   Signed K. ФАБЕРЖЕ

R22 CAVIAR SCOOP, in striated brown agate with a dull yellow gold handle chased with concentric circles narrowing to a globe set with five cabochon sapphires. [122]
Length 5⅜ inches   Signed EK
Gold mark crossed anchors

R44

R23 Bowenite HANDLE of crook form, with a red gold collar enamelled with a Greek key pattern in opaque white against a background of translucent scarlet enamel over engraving, enclosed between two borders of rose diamonds. Removable modern silver-gilt blade by Tom Scott. [122]
Height 2⅛ inches   Signed MΠ

R24 Bowenite HANDLE set with two carbuncles and mounted with a reeded red gold collar chased with green gold laurel borders, enamelled translucent rust over *moiré* engine-turning. Removable modern silver-gilt blade by Tom Scott. [122]
Height 1 15/16 inches   Signed MΠ
Gold mark crossed anchors

R21 to **R24**, Wartski, London.

R25 Dark sherry agate NEGRO'S HEAD, the face finished matt, the lips polished and with rose diamond eyes set in yellow gold, each composed of a single stone set between two smaller. Hollowed out as a bowl with a red and yellow gold rim chased with Vitruvian scrolls; when held up to the light, this skilfully carved object imparts an attractive golden glow. [123]
Height 2 3/16 inches   Signed MΠ
Gold mark crossed anchors   AKS plate 274

R26 Tiny carving of a PIG in translucent pale pinky-brown chalcedony with a tawny patch on one side and set with rose diamond eyes.
Length ⅞ inch

R27 Amazonite carving of the THREE WISE MONKEYS combined in a single oviform netsuke.
Height 1 3/16 inches
AKS colour plate XXXIV

(enlarged)   **R27**

R28 Grey Kalgan jasper ELEPHANT with rose diamond eyes.
Length 1⅛ inches
AKS colour plate XXXIV

R29 Speckled brown and black jasper BULL-DOG, set with rose diamond eyes foiled green. He stands glowering with Churchillian defiance.
Length 3⅛ inches

R30 A bowenite carving of an ELEPHANT, poised on its front legs and trunk, set with cabochon ruby eyes.
Height 1½ inches

R31 GIANT ANT-EATER in banded agate in tones of brown, set with rose diamond eyes.
Length 3 5/16 inches
AKS colour plate XLIX

R31

R32 Bloodstone carving of a seated PELICAN with rose diamond eyes set in gold.
Length 1¾ inches

R33 Pale brown chalcedony SEATED KITTEN with cabochon ruby eyes.
Height 1¾ inches
AKS plate 106

R34 Grey chalcedony carving of a CAT having pounced, set with rose diamond eyes.
Length 2¾ inches
AKS plate 106

R34, R33

R35 Vari-coloured agate seated OSTRICH, with chased gold legs and set with green garnet eyes.
Length 2⅜ inches   Signed HW

R36 CHIMPANZEE seated upon a stool carved from a single piece of vari-coloured jasper, and set with brilliant-cut diamond eyes.
Height 2½ inches

R37 Gold ÉTUI-A-CIRE of oval section, enamelled translucent pale pink enriched with indigo foliate trelliswork and split pearls, gold borders set with rose diamonds and an intaglio matrix.
Length 5 inches   Signed МП

R38 BELL-PUSH designed as a sphinx, in lapis lazuli and set with diamonds and rubies, reclining on a gold base with a chased scrolling border and enamelled opalescent oyster on a *guilloché* field.
Length 4⅜ inches   Signed К. ФАБЕРЖЕ
AKS plate 176

enamelled *champlevé*. The oval ends set with moss-agates foiled rose within rose diamond borders, and the pushpiece is composed of a crown rose diamond. The interior is divided into compartments and contains a looking-glass and a reeded gold lipstick holder.
Length 3½ inches   Signed HW
Gold mark 72

R40 Engraved red gold square STRUT FRAME standing on one corner, enamelled pale translucent cinnamon over an engraved sunray ground, the circular aperture edged with half-pearls. The little girl in the photograph appears to be Princess Nina Georgievna of Russia, the daughter of Grand Duke George Mikhailovich and Princess Marie of Greece.
3 inches square   Signed HW
Mr P. C. Hegard, Norway.

R36

R38

R39 Combined gold CIGARETTE CASE AND POWDER BOX of tubular form enamelled bright translucent orange over a *guilloché* ground, reserved with elongated opaque black stripes

OPPOSITE *Left* O21 *Right* R2 OVERLEAF ▼

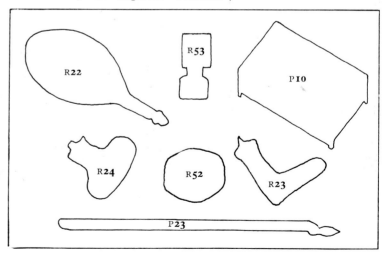

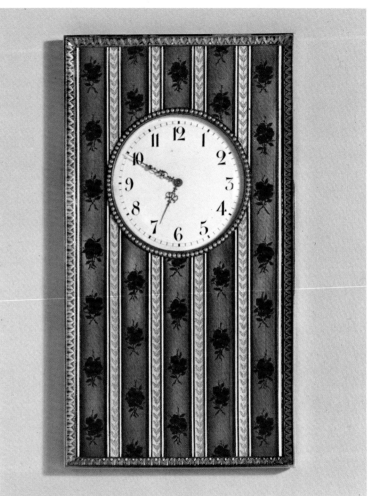

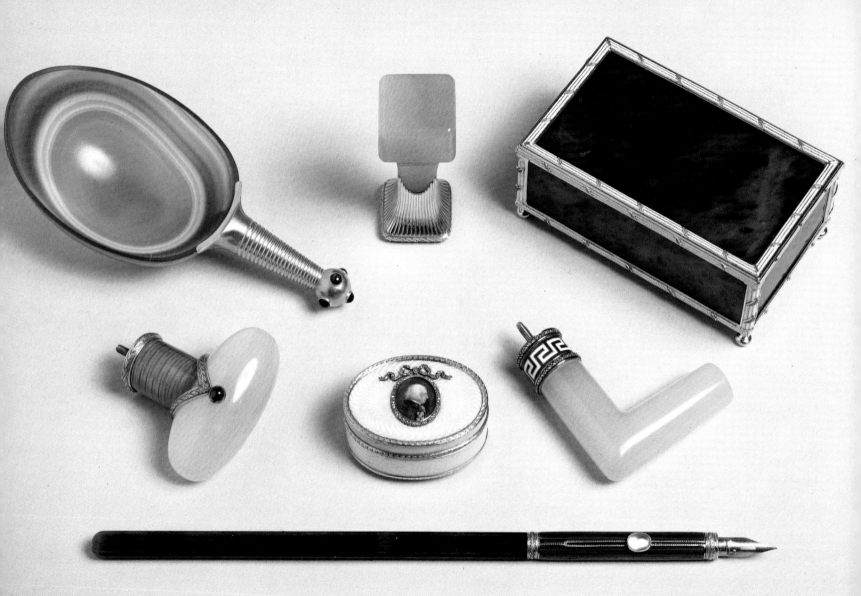

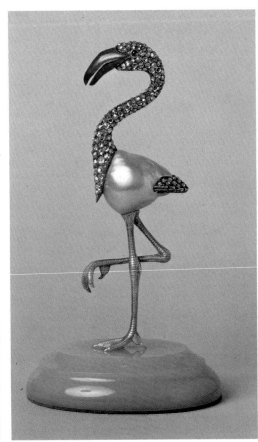

124 ▷

R41 Oviform red gold STRUT FRAME, bordered by chased dull green gold laurel and enamelled translucent strawberry over a radiating engraving, with a carved bowenite area round the oval beaded gold aperture.
Height 4¼ inches   Signed MΠ
Gold mark crossed anchors

R42 Oval silver-gilt STRUT FRAME surmounted by a yellow gold bow-knot, enamelled translucent deep yellow over a radiating engine-turning within a raised border of green translucent enamelled leaves over engraved veining, each leaf reserved with a gold outline. The frame is richly decorated with trails of roses chased in green, red and white gold. An unusually early example of Fabergé's work in this genre. It contains a highly finished painting in tempera of a young girl, partly clothed in a diaphanous veiling and wearing a pearl and gold chain necklace and a triple bandeau of hoops. Presumably the framed portrait was privately commissioned by an admirer.
Height 5¼ inches
Signed К. ФАБЕРЖЕ and dated Moscow 1896

R43 Chased red gold rectangular miniature STRUT FRAME, surmounted by a bow-knotted ribbon and standing upon two feet, enamelled translucent sky-blue over an engraved field applied with chased dull green gold trails of leaves and berries, set with four half pearls, with a broad inner margin enamelled opalescent oyster over engraving bordering the oval aperture.
Height 2½ inches   Signed BA

R44 Rectangular dull green gold FRAME, the borders of concave section ribbed with a sunray pattern, the engraved mount echoes this motif and is enamelled opalescent oyster. The octagonal aperture, with an engraved red gold border, contains a painted miniature portrait of the Emperor Napoleon in uniform.
Height 1⅝ inches   Signed MΠ

R45 Rhodonite CASKET mounted in yellow gold, the hinged cover bordered by opaque white and translucent emerald enamel pellets and rosettes and mounted with a rose diamond thumb-piece; it stands on four ball feet enamelled with stripes in the same palette.
Length 2⅜ inches   Signed HW
Gold mark 72
AKS colour plate XIII

R46 Small oval engraved yellow gold BOX, enamelled overall translucent royal blue on engraved fields, the surfaces divided into stripes by engraved gold bands, the hinged lid mounted with a chased green gold foliate bezel, an outer border of half-pearls and a miniature painting of a young girl after Greuze within a frame of brilliant diamonds.
Length 1 9/16 inches   Signed MΠ
Gold mark 72
AKS colour plate XIII

R47 Oval BONBONNIÈRE in engraved red gold enamelled opaque white, the *bombé* sides with groups of three fine gold dotted lines between broader engraved bands meeting under the box round a reserved oval area of gold. The hinged cover is set with a fine 17th century dark brown, grey-blue and cream agate cameo within a rose diamond frame, depicting Aurora

OVERLEAF   *Left* ▼   *Right* Q3   OPPOSITE S19

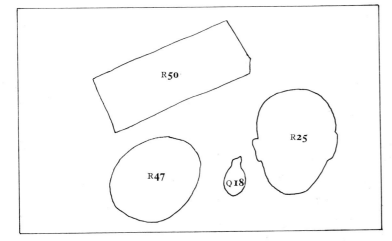

in her biga (chariot) driving two horses through the clouds. [123]
Length 2 inches   Signed MΠ
Gold mark crossed anchors

R48 Rectangular hinged BOX carved in bowenite, with red and green gold chased laurel bezel set with a rose diamond thumb-piece.
Length 2 inches   Signed ΦA
AKS colour plate XIII

R49 Yellow gold heart-shaped BOX, the sides enamelled opalescent oyster on a diapered ground, the base and the removable cover both set with carved and bevelled rock crystal panels edged by rose diamonds.
Length 1 $\frac{9}{16}$ inches   Signed HW
Gold mark 72
AKS colour plate XIII

R50 Burnished red gold hinged rectangular BOX, with bevelled borders decorated with dull green gold acanthus leaves, the sides enamelled translucent emerald green over *moiré* engraving, the top and bottom of the box are set with carved rhodonite panels. Both the enamelled and stone panels are bordered by an opaque white enamelled line and the thumb-piece is set with rose diamonds. [123]
Length 3 $\frac{3}{8}$ inches   Signed HW
Gold mark 72

R51 Octagonal jasper BOX, mounted in red gold with chased green gold laurel swags round the sides suspended from a rose diamond border. The hinged cover is applied with a trophy composed of a red gold bow and arrow and a garland of leaves and berries chased in green gold.
Width 1 $\frac{1}{2}$ inches   Signed MΠ
Madame Josiane Woolf, France.

R52 Oval silver BOX, mounted in engraved red gold with two chased green gold foliate borders, enamelled overall opalescent oyster over wavy engine-turning, the hinged cover applied with an eighteenth century oval miniature painting of the Count Besborodko, Catherine the Great's scribe, wearing his Orders, within a narrow frame of rose diamonds surmounted by a bow-knot. [122]
Length 1 $\frac{7}{8}$ inches   Signed HW

R53 Bowenite HAND-SEAL, with a simple reeded red gold mount bordered by a chased green gold foliate mount. [122]
Height 2 $\frac{1}{2}$ inches   Signed MΠ

R52 and R53, Wartski, London.

R54 GOLD BOX in the form of a die, with faceted corners, the hinged lid skilfully concealed, each of the sides, enamelled translucent royal blue over a sunburst *guilloché* ground, is set with one to six rose diamonds in the traditional pattern. [82]
1 $\frac{3}{16}$ inches square   Signed MΠ

R55 Circular POWDER BOX, enamelled translucent deep magenta on a *moiré* ground with borders of opaque white and chased leaf and berry motifs, heightened with black enamel.
Diameter 2 $\frac{1}{2}$ inches   Signed HW
AKS colour plate XIV
Mrs Emanuel Snowman, London

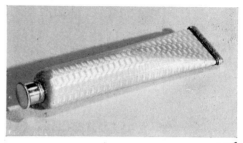

R56

R56 Silver SCENT FLACON in the form of a tube of tooth-paste, with chased gold mounts, enamelled translucent pale blue over an engraved ground.
Length 2 $\frac{3}{4}$ inches   No marks
AKS plate 175
Duchess of Devonshire, Chatsworth

R57 Rock crystal circular BONBONNIÈRE, divided into six pearl-shaped lobes each containing an engraved winged cupid. The hinged lid is enamelled opalescent champagne over an engraved romantic trophy composed of bow, arrows and quiver within a border of leaves and flowerheads edged by an opaque white enamelled line and rose diamonds culminating in an elaborate thumb-piece. Another white line encircles the top of the box which is itself engraved with scrolls and foliage. [82]
Diameter 1 $\frac{11}{16}$ inches
Signed HW
Gold mark 72

CASE S

S1 Three chased silver-gilt peacocks form the base supporting a TIFFANY GLASS VASE decorated with peacock feather motifs. The vase was given by Louis C. Tiffany to Miss Julia Grant, daughter of General Grant, and Prince Michael Cantacuzene on the occasion of their wedding at the White House, where the bride was born. Later, when the couple lived in Russia, Fabergé was commissioned to design the mount.
Overall height 7¾ inches   Mount signed BA

S2 LAMP with Lötz glass body of opalescent silver and orange lighting from within. The silver-gilt mounts matching the figuration in the glass, are chased with wave and foliate motifs to suggest the sea; four dolphins form the base. This *art nouveau* object is from the Royal Yacht *Standart*.
Height (excluding shade) 11 inches
Signed BA

S3 TIFFANY GLASS JAR mounted in oxidised silver and set with pearls. A striking example of *art nouveau* by Fabergé.
Height 4⅛ inches   Signed BA
AKS plate 58

S1, S2 and S3, Herr A. F. Harmstorf, Hamburg.

S4 Oxidised silver four-piece TEA SERVICE in Moorish taste, gilded within, chased with plaited meander and conventionalized leaf borders and geometric pattern handles embossed with large studs.
Height of water jug 8¼ inches   Signed SW
Silver mark St Petersburg 1888

S5 Silver-gilt and *cloisonné*-enamelled VASE, with, on one side, a painting of Fabergé's Moscow shop showing his name-board under the Imperial Eagle, and, on the other, an inscription reading: 'xxv To the highly esteemed Carl Gustavovich in gratitude F. I. Ruckert 1912'. This presumably indicates that the Moscow German had worked for Fabergé since 1887. The vase itself is decorated with stylized flowers and fruit in the pastel colours characteristic of the maker's work.
Height 4½ inches   Signed ФР
A la Vieille Russie, New York.

S6 Silver KOVSH, gilt within, and enamelled overall matt Wedgwood blue and reserved with a pattern of *repoussé* scrolls and pellets and set with a cabochon ruby on the handle.
Length 4 7/16 inches   Signed К. ФАБЕРЖЕ
Mr and Mrs E. Amirkhamian, Tehran.

S7 An ingeniously designed PORTRAIT in silver of IVAN KALITA, the celebrated folk hero and miser. He is modelled as a moneybag (*Kalita*) in the Old Russian style; the model is set with

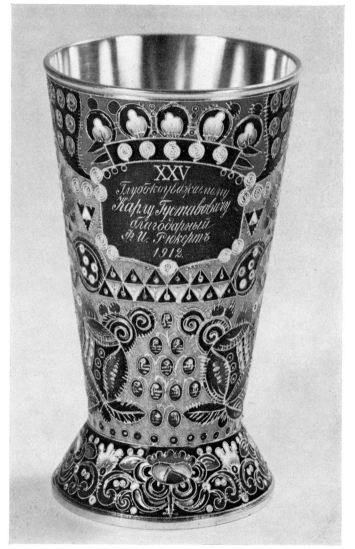

S5

S5

S7

Length 8 $\frac{3}{16}$ inches Signed BA
Silver mark crossed anchors

s9 Shaped BELL-PUSH intended as a panel for
the wall in holly wood with silver-gilt mounts
in Louis XVI style, similar to the previous
exhibit, and also with a moonstone push.
Length 5 $\frac{15}{16}$ inches

S10 TALLOW-BURNER in the form of a European
green lizard naturalistically chased and engraved in silver and set with cabochon ruby
eyes. The head is removable to allow the wick
to be packed into the interior; when lit it
emerges as a flaming tongue.
Length 7 inches Signed IP

s8, s9 and S10, Dr Edwin I. Radlauer, New
York.

S11 CIGARETTE CASE in palisander wood with a
reeded red gold mount and hung with dull

two cabochon emeralds and a ruby and is
gilded within. Ivan Moneybag, who reigned
from 1328 to 1341, was the first of the Gatherers
of the Lands of Russia, Grand Dukes of
Moscovy who united the feudal states, the last
of whom was Ivan the Terrible. Despite his
miserly reputation, it is traditionally held that
he nonetheless gave alms to the poor.
Height 6 $\frac{1}{2}$ inches Signed K. ФАБЕРЖЕ
Mr Irving M. Feldstein, Chicago

s8 Rectangular BELL-PUSH designed as a wall
panel in palisander wood, applied with chased
oxidised silver mounts, an arrow with a moonstone push at its centre in a gadrooned border
and two intertwined trails of berried leaves, all
within a chased border.

green gold chased foliate swags with burnished
red gold folds of drapery falling from four bow-
knots each set with a moonstone, one of which
serves as push-piece.
Length 3 $\frac{9}{16}$ inches Signed BA

S12 Silver-gilt VODKA CUP, in the form of a
miniature helmet of the Imperial Horse Guard
with the enamelled silver Badge and Star of
the Order of St Andrew, surmounted by a
chased silver crowned Imperial Eagle.
Height 5 $\frac{3}{8}$ inches Signed AH
Silver mark crossed anchors

S13 Silver samorodok CIGARETTE CASE, gilded
within and mounted with a gold thumb-piece
set with a cabochon ruby. Fabergé pioneered
this interesting technique whereby the surface
of silver or gold took on a rough molten quality
giving the object the appearance of a nugget
(samorodok). It was obtained by bringing the

S10

129

S12

S15

S15 A chased and engraved silver SNAKE, curled round a large turquoise matrix.
Width 7¼ inches   Signed BA
Mr and Mrs Nigel Broackes, London.

S16 Copper SAUCEPAN AND COVER with brass handles. An example of the sort of practical objects the House made as part of the war effort. Engraved with the Russian word for *War* and the year 1914.
Height 5 inches   Signed К. ФАБЕРЖЕ
From the India Early Minshall collection of the Cleveland Museum of Art, U.S.A.

S17 Rectangular silver FRAME, partly gilt with a border chased with Vitruvian scrolls, enamelled opalescent oyster over sunray engraving round the oval aperture. Overlaid with two sprays of chased and engraved silver Madonna lilies each tied with a pale green translucent enamelled knotted ribbon.
Height 7¼ inches   Signed BA

S18 Circular bottle-green glazed pottery BOWL, the interior fluted, with a reeded silver

mount incorporating two handles composed of chased wreaths with ribbons. [124]
Overall length 5⅛ inches   Signed AN

S17 and S18, Mr and Mrs E. Amirkhanian, Tehran.

metal plate almost up to melting point and then deftly removing it from the fire. The sudden cooler temperature shrank the plate and gave it the desired rumpled finish.
Length 3⅞ inches   Signed АГ

S14 A fantastic BIRD in a fine-grained sandstone with chased silver mounts and carbuncle eyes. Designed as a holder for matches to be struck on the stone, this curiosity by Fabergé appears to have strayed from Hieronymous Bosch's 'Garden of Delights', a forerunner of so many dreaded seaside tourist souvenirs.
Length 5½ inches   Signed IP
Silver mark crossed anchors
AKS plate 55
Mr Robert Rush, Los Angeles.

S14

S19 Twelve silver-gilt SPOONS, each one of a different design and *cloisonné* enamelled in a different pattern in a range of pastel colours. These spoons are a good example of the muted palette preferred by Fabergé in favour of the more garish colours, such as a piercing sky blue, used by contemporary Russian enamellers. The lid lining of the spoons case is of interest indicating where the firm was in business. Not only are Moscow, St Petersburg, Kiev, Odessa and London listed but also, Nijegor Yarmar (abbreviation of Nijegor Rodskaya Yarmarka). This was the commercial section of Nijni Novgorod where a vast annual fair was held and in which Fabergé presumably took part. [124]

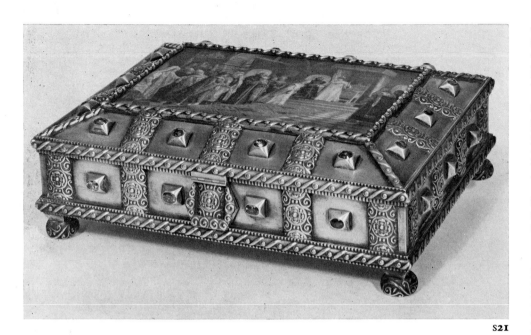

S21

Lengths ranging from $4\frac{9}{16}$ inches to $4\frac{3}{4}$ inches
Signed РФ and overstruck К. ФАБЕРЖЕ
Mr and Mrs Edward Joseph, Tehran

S20 Circular *bombé* silver BOX, the hinged top ribbed with triple bands radiating from a Catherine the Great medallion dated 1786 and enamelled translucent yellow round the profile of the Empress. The gold thumb-piece is set with a carbuncle.
Diameter $2\frac{3}{4}$ inches
Signed К. ФАБЕРЖЕ together with the initials AR an unknown workmaster in either Odessa or Kiev.
See AKS page 128
Andrew H. Lane Paneyko, New Jersey.

S21 Oxidised chased silver CASKET, in the seventeenth century Russian manner (the Old Russian Style) set with blue, yellow and brown sapphires. In the cover is set an enamelled painting after Constantine Makovsky's masterpiece in the Tretiakov Gallery, Moscow, by Haritonov. It depicts the traditional selection of a bride for the Tsar in the sixteenth century. One of the objects made during the 1913 Romanov Tercentenary celebrations.
Length $7\frac{7}{8}$ inches   Signed К. ФАБЕРЖЕ
AKS plate 63

S22 Rectangular silver-gilt double-opening CIGARETTE CASE, with rounded corners, enamelled overall translucent pale lavender over an engraved sunburst ground, applied on the front with a rose diamond-set Imperial eagle of Nicholas I and fitted with a rose-diamond push-piece.
Length 4 inches   Signed A★H

S23 Silver CIGARETTE BOX decorated with *niello* work – an extremely rare example of Fabergé's use of this technique.
Length $3\frac{1}{4}$ inches   Signed К. ФАБЕРЖЕ
HCB plate 116   AKS plate 94
Mr A. Kenneth Snowman, London.

S24 Travelling INK POT, of cube form in reeded silver, the swivel catch set with a cabochon sapphire push-piece. Engraved inside:

Natalie
22 November 1915 Gatchina

Natalie refers to the Countess Brassov who had a morganatic marriage with the Grand Duke Michael Alexandrovitch and lived at Gatchina.
Height $2\frac{5}{8}$ inches
Signed BC and also signed К. ФАБЕРЖЕ indicating that Soloviev, like A. Navalainen sometimes worked away from St Petersburg, possibly in Moscow.
Herr Fritz Attinger, Zurich.

★   ★   ★

In addition to the items catalogued, the Exhibition includes the wax models for a stallion and a guinea pig originally in the possession of H. C. Bainbridge, a number of designs for jewels, relevant documents and photographs of the workshops and premises.

A bust of Queen Alexandra in marble by H. Garland and kindly lent by the National Portrait Gallery, stands in a niche at the entrance to the Exhibition.

Group of Fabergé cases in holly wood and the velvet covered case for
the Lilies of the Valley Egg (02).